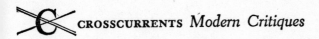

CROSSCURRENTS *Modern Critiques*

CROSSCURRENTS *Modern Critiques*
Harry T. Moore, *General Editor*

Oscar Cargill

Toward
a Pluralistic Criticism

WITH A PREFACE BY

Harry T. Moore

Carbondale and Edwardsville

SOUTHERN ILLINOIS UNIVERSITY PRESS

To My Colleagues
in the
All-University Department of English
NEW YORK UNIVERSITY

PREFACE

OSCAR CARGILL has for many years been chairman of New York University's all-university English department, which he has built into one of the finest teaching units in the country. And he has himself been a remarkable teacher, particularly in his famous course devoted to James and Eliot. He has also managed to be a first-rate writer, as the essays in this book will show. In addition he has edited various anthologies and is the author of such volumes as Intellectual America, Thomas Wolfe at Washington Square, and The Novels of Henry James.

In his brief Introduction to the present book, Mr. Cargill explains how he grew into pluralistic criticism, and in his first essay (which has the same title as this volume) he defines the subject itself, as part of an illuminating survey of recent criticism. He has seen the so-called new critics come and go, and he values the contribution they made in calling the reader's attention to what the author had actually written; but eventually they produced a method of treating literature as if it existed in a vacuum, and this method couldn't, didn't, endure. As Mr. Cargill sees the matter, the commentator on literature must be a critic, and as much a critic as any of the so-called new ones were, and he must also be a scholar. He makes these points with quiet authority and comprehensive judiciousness.

The essays which follow show pluralistic criticism in action, chiefly in relation to American authors. The range is wide, from Whitman to his quite different contemporary,

Henry Adams; from Frank Norris to T. S. Eliot; from William Dean Howells to Hart Crane; from the James family to H. L. Mencken. These essays, appearing in periodicals, have across the years earned themselves an appropriate amount of fame as single units; now it is a pleasure to find them gathered together in this book, for they represent a kind of superior criticism. The last of these essays, "Mass Media and Literature," has not been published before. It is sternly critical of the type of reviewing which appears in American newspapers and the attempts of television to present drama between the battering of commercials; yet this essay has a final paragraph, written several years after the main part, which sounds a note of hope.

Mr. Cargill's own work doesn't appear in mass media, but those of us who have been associated with bringing out the present volume hope that it will give Mr. Cargill's stimulating and important essays wider currency among those who buy quality books at a price as low as volumes in the present series can be kept. Mr. Cargill's pluralistic approach will enlarge any reader's knowledge of and response to literature, in the most creative way possible, for Oscar Cargill believes that criticism is creative, that it increases not only the understanding of literature but its very values. His essays convincingly show why.

HARRY T. MOORE

Southern Illinois University
March 4, 1965

ACKNOWLEDGMENTS

TOWARD A PLURALISTIC CRITICISM was first printed in the Commencement Program of New York University, June 10, 1964, and is reprinted by arrangement with the University.

WALT WHITMAN AND HIS LEAVES OF GRASS is the "Introduction" to Harper's Modern Classics edition of *Leaves of Grass*, Copyright, 1950, by Harper and Brothers. Reprinted by permission of Harper & Row, Publishers.

THE MEDIEVALISM OF HENRY ADAMS is from *Essays and Studies in Honor of Carleton Brown*, Copyright, 1940, New York University Press. Reprinted by permission of the New York University Press. Extended quotation is made in the essay from copyrighted material by permission of the following: from *The Education of Henry Adams*, from *Mont-Saint-Michel and Chartres*, from *The Letters of Henry Adams* and *A Cycle of Adams Letters* (both edited by Worthington Chauncey Ford), from *Charles Francis Adams: An Autobiography*, and from *Letters to a Niece* and *Prayer to the Virgin of Chartres* by the Houghton Mifflin Company; from *The Letters of Mrs. Henry Adams* (edited by Ward Thoron) by Mrs. Ward Thoron and by Little, Brown and Company.

WILLIAM DEAN HOWELLS AS HENRY JAMES'S "MORAL POLICEMAN" appeared as "Henry James's 'Moral Policeman': William Dean Howells" in *American Literature*, XXIX, No. 4 (January, 1958), 371–98, and is reprinted by permission of the copyright holder, the Duke University Press.

THE TURN OF THE SCREW AND ALICE JAMES is reprinted by permission of the Modern Language Association from *PMLA*, LXXVIII (June, 1963), 238–49.

A ROBBER BARON REVISES THE OCTOPUS is the "Afterword" to the Signet Classics edition of *The Octopus*. Copyright, 1964, by The New American Library of World Literature, Inc., and reprinted by permission of the publisher.

MENCKEN AND THE SOUTH appeared in *The Georgia Review*, VI, No. 4 (Winter, 1952), 369–76, and is reprinted by permission of *The Georgia Review*.

ANATOMIST OF MONSTERS is reprinted with the permission of the National Council of Teachers of English from *College English*, October, 1947, issue.

HART CRANE IN LIMBO is reprinted from two sources, both in copyright:

"Hart Crane and His Friends" is reprinted from *The Nation*, Vol. 186 (15 February 1958), 142–43, by permission of *The Nation* and its publisher, George G. Kirstein.

"The 'Unfractioned Idiom' of *The Bridge*" is a review reprinted from *Poetry* magazine for June, 1961, by permission of *Poetry*.

MR. ELIOT REGRETS . . . is reprinted from *The Nation*, Vol. 184 (23 February 1957), 170–172, by permission of *The Nation* and its publisher, George G. Kirstein, holders of the copyright.

POETRY SINCE THE DELUGE is reprinted with the permission of the National Council of Teachers of English from *College English*, February, 1954, issue.

MASS MEDIA AND LITERATURE is here printed for the first time.

I wish especially to acknowledge help given me at various times in these essays and in the preparation of this book by the following persons: Gay Wilson Allen, Dorothy Alyea, Louise Azzato, Walter Brackman, Leon Edel, William M. Gibson, Clarence Gohdes, William B. Harvey, Robert Hatch, Wilbur Hatfield, Max J. Herzberg, Frederick J. Hoffman, John H. Langley, Percy Long, Edward L. McAdam, Jr., James E. Miller, Harry T.

Moore, John Frederick Nims, Edd Winfield Parks, Thomas Clark Pollock, Henry Rago, David Ray, Macha Rosenthal, Ann Shankland, Henry Nash Smith, Priscilla C. Smith, and George Winchester Stone, Jr. Acceptance of these essays in their original place of issue strangely encountered in many instances both secret and open opposition. I honor those persons in the above list who effectively pulled an oar for their publication so that I did not have to peddle them about.

CONTENTS

INTRODUCTION

I HAVE ALWAYS HELD that any method which could produce the meaning of a work of literature was a legitimate method. After completing *Intellectual America*, which I did not regard as a work of criticism but rather as a history of ideologies, I was engaged for a time on research for subsequent volumes. Suddenly I was drawn into administration and faced with the absorbing task of creating a distinguished department of English, an assignment that called upon talents as varied as those of an accountant, a ward boss, a baseball scout, and an impressario. Fortunately, this kept me out of the critical discussions and controversies that, during two decades, forged different sharp tools for the practice of criticism. Nevertheless, I continued to write occasional essays, seizing any convenient method in a search for the author's meaning. It was only toward the end of my exacting administrative assignment that I began to think seriously about the problems of criticism. Whether from re-reading much later things I myself had written and being puzzled over what I had intended or from the answers of established authors when questions were put to them similar to the one I put to myself, and getting sense out of their generally whimsical replies ("Young lady, when I wrote that, only God and I knew what I meant, but now only God knows"), I came to the conclusion that, after all, the critic's task was not to get the author's meaning (for even if the author lived and was voluble, there was small chance of that), but to procure a viable meaning appropriate to the critic's time and place. Practically, this meant employing not any one method in interpreting a work of art but every method which might prove efficient. If all of those used led to the same interpretation, that interpretation, if not immediately a viable meaning, would shortly become one. It was a delight to me, when I turned again to interpretation, to discover what a great variety of methods had been matured during my distracted years and I did not have to invent any. The first genuine application I made of a pluralistic approach is in some of the essays I published prior to writing *The Novels of Henry James*. The developing experience of this "late blooming" critic is written over the face of the essays in this volume. The "Afterword" generally reflects on the limitations of each endeavor, for the sake of those interested in method. But I may be permitted to hope that the substance of some of my exercises will win a little attention. In summary, let me report I have made for myself a discovery as to the importance of criticism. Whereas I had always regarded it as a secondary, subservient art, though capable of brilliant execution in the right hands, through reflection on the meaning of meaning, I have come to the conclusion it is a primary art. Without a viable meaning, a creative writer has no significance; he cannot achieve it himself, unless he turns to criticism—it is the critics who endow art with meaning.

OSCAR CARGILL

January, 1965

Toward a Pluralistic Criticism

1   TOWARD A PLURALISTIC CRITICISM

THE FUNCTION of the critic and scholar is to make the past functional, for unless it can be used, it is deader than death itself. The only alternative is to adopt the view of Antoine Roquetin, Jean-Paul Sartre's non-hero, that the past has no existence, a thesis which does more than alienate him from bourgeoise society—it negates all continuity, all history, all culture and renders scholarship and criticism impotent. Such an assault on animal wisdom, however, compels definition, or at least description. What is the past? Where does it begin and where does it end? Psychologists and philosophers enforce the presentness of the past by telling us that by the time our very inadequate perceptive apparatus reports an event it is already historic, and the very notion of the present is a conventional fiction. The past is time, or what we live in. The slippery present is that which has too much concerned the existentialists, certainly emotionally; but a paradoxical love of books shows how easy it would be to accept time or continuity. To emend Descartes, from whom they really take their being, "I think, therefore I exist *in time*." With any sense of the all-enveloping past one cannot be a complete disaffiliate.

In literature, ostensibly, the great generation of the twenties exhibited the fullest sort of consciousness of continuity: *Remembrance of Things Past, Ulysses, The Waste Land, Look Homeward, Angel,* all seemed to be documents in support of the affirmation of the ever-presence of the past. Such, doubtless, their authors intended them to be, but was that saliently their effect? Loneliness and alienation are themes in each of them; analogues, parallels, symbols, and metaphors from the past in each one of them are lost in the dubious hero's swamping, dismal present. Did not they prepare the way for Camus, Sartre, Ionesco, and Duerrenmatt? Did not much that transpired in intellectual circles, in education, prepare the way? Reverence for the past was undermined in the academies in the twenties and thirties. Ancient history and Latin disappeared from the lower schools; today, anything resembling the orderly presentation of English and American literature in the colleges is following after. Much is said of the virtue of studying only masterpieces, but when the *Iliad* jostles *The Divine Comedy*, and the latter, *King Lear*, all sense of time is lost, and these masterpieces become companion works to *Crime and Punishment* and *Death in Venice*, if not to *Catcher in the Rye* and *Herzog*. In the ingenious presentations of instructors who confine themselves to the work itself, that is, the work in a modern translation, these masterpieces take on a contemporaneity scarcely achieved by the latest novel. Virgil in *The Divine Comedy*, like Ulysses before him, becomes a father image and Achilles, sulking in his tent, is a symbol of onanism. But alas, when so old-fashioned a person as I makes what he thinks is an illuminating comparison between *The Rime of the Ancient Mariner* and *The Waste Land*, he is met by blank stares—only four persons in the class have read Coleridge's poem. It has been relegated, possibly, to a deeper past than the *Iliad*. Thus the most valuable element in time, the sense of continuity, the sense of having a tradition, is lost for the young.

Our appropriation of the master works of the West seems to have more in common with the indiscriminate accumulations of the newspaper millionaire, William Randolph Hearst, than with the slow and painful assimilations of Bernard Berenson. We rape from frame and setting to adorn our own tales or to trigger a specious erudition. Unlike Hearst, however, we are very cautious not to carry away too much. This caution came from the vice of the previous age, when American literary scholarship reached a peak in the work of E. K. Rand, George Lyman Kittredge, Carleton Brown, W. W. Lawrence, Edwin Greenlaw, and others. The enormous erudition of these scholars, their supersaturation with the past, staggered and baffled younger minds until they made a liberating discovery—in the interest of frame and setting, in the interest of biography, their teachers were neglecting the work of art itself or burying it under mounds of "useless knowledge" from which it never could be excavated. The sensitive and intuitive John Livingston Lowes, author of *Convention and Revolt in Poetry*, undertook to correct the balance in *The Road to Xanadu*, but he was much too late. As early as 1920 T. S. Eliot was proclaiming that the essential critical function is "elucidation," not of the artist but of the work of art. The revolt against the *impedimenta* of scholarship went so far that it actually detached the artist from his creation. "Never trust the artist, trust the tale," declared D. H. Lawrence. The most iconoclastic position reached in this revolt is that of Marcel Proust in *Contre Sainte-Beuve*, in which Proust ridiculed all attempts to document the life of an author, asserting that quite a different ego produces the work of art from the ego which inhabits the common walks of life. A similar extremism severed the work of art from the "past" of its creation. "To appreciate a work of art," wrote Clive Bell, "we need bring with us nothing from life, no knowledge of its ideas and affairs, no familiarity with its emotions." Of the masterpiece, A. C. Bradley declared, "Its nature is not to be a part, nor a copy of the real world . . . , but a world in itself, independent, complete, autonomous."

Having separated the masterpiece from its creator and from its place in time, the new critic concentrated with great intensity upon elucidating the text itself. He found, we may infer from Cleanth Brooks, that he had to address an audience which could not read, since neglect of the masterpiece for facts about it and its author had caused the faculty of apprehension to atrophy. With John Crowe Ransom, Allen Tate, Robert Penn Warren, R. P. Blackmur, and others, Mr. Brooks set out to remedy this defect. That the method which they championed, *explication de texte,* had long been employed at the high school level in France, in the *lycée,* is no condemnation if it: very elementary beginnings had to be made. Whether "dry-as-dust" scholarship was responsible for general illiteracy or (as I think) neglect of composition (which forces attention on the text) in the lower schools is immaterial, *Americans could not read.* Even the errors made by some of the explicators only substantiate the fact. Regardless of whether or not the methods of the new critics provided a richer appreciation, it must be granted that they accomplished a major miracle—they taught some few Americans to read.

One of the announced aims of the new critic was not to interpose his own personality between the reader and the work itself. He saw that this was the equivalent, if not worse, of allowing the workaday ego of the author to interpose. The critic would deny his own ego, his hunger for recognition, for the ideal end of perfectly interpreting the text before him. Granted the human condition, however, he was utterly incapable of achieving this end. Yet it is important that we note its unearthly character, its metaphysical nature. Only a writer completely cut off from the world, only a perpetual dweller among masterpieces, only an academic—such as all new critics became—could utter such nonsense and, at least partially, believe it. For only the universities provided the proper pasturage for this kind of gamboling and, lest weeds and underbrush get in, the new critics in the main concentrated on the classics of the literature of the past, erecting stiles against current literature. F. R. Leavis, the Cambridge don who founded a magazine to scrutinize texts and kept it going for twenty years, illustrated the impossibility of a depersonalized criticism operating upon a depersonalized literature—he created a school of *obita dictarists* who ever looked anxiously to him for the Word. In the main, the new critics found that the first principles they had drawn up were narrow and stultifying and, without announcing it, they one after another abandoned them. It has been said that Cleanth Brooks is the only remaining new critic, the only one tenaciously attached to the text. The others have adopted a variety of methods: they have specialized in aesthetic structure, sociological background, morals, psychology, and myths—each, however, a champion of his own special method.

Meanwhile, although crowded into the more stony part of the pasture, and scarcely visible over the high fences, research scholars in the universities had continued to exist. Indeed, in the very years when the new criticism rocked the academies, research scholarship recorded some of its most remarkable achievements. Almost anyone can enumerate a few examples of literary scholarship that seem to be more perdurable than anything produced by the whole corps of new critics: the editing of the *Diaries* of Samuel Johnson by Edward L. McAdam, Jr., and of Thackeray's *Letters* by Gordon Ray, *The Young Shelley* by Kenneth Cameron, and the study of the mind of Walt Whitman by Gay Allen. What in the new criticism can compare with Perry Miller's investigations of Puritan culture, Thomas H. Johnson's detective work in determining the text and order of Emily Dickinson's poetry, Jay Leyda's *The Melville Log*, the editions of the letters of Pope, Keats, Coleridge, and George Eliot by George Sherburn, Hyder Rollins, Earl Griggs, and Gordon Haight, respectively, and the astonishing critical life of James Joyce by Richard Ellmann? From their labors the scholars occasionally turned aside to expose gleefully the limitations of a new criticism that depended largely on impressionism, intuition, clairvoyance, and extrasensory perception. Douglas Bush had most sport at this and delighted his colleagues. Who can forget his definition of the new criticism as "an advanced course in remedial reading"? When John Crowe Ransom wondered over Shakespeare's use of the phrase "dusty death," calling it "an odd but winning detail," Bush reminded him that the same odd but winning detail is in the Bible and *The Book of Common Prayer*, with which Shakespeare was doubtless familiar. Lillian Hornstein deflated some of the pretentiousness of Caroline Spurgeon's *Shakespeare's Imagery*, an offshoot of the new criticism, in much the same way.

Though the scholars scored heavily off the critics, they themselves found the new criticism properly admonitory. Scholars wish today to be taken also for critics, and with justice they may so be regarded, for they at last have learned to emphasize the creations of the artist above his sources, background, and life, while retaining illumination from the latter. The critics, on the other hand, because they have confined their work to classics and have found the newest classics ever receding into the past, are coming more and more to respect biography and history and to take simple excursions into them. Because of their academic associations some of them undeniably have discovered it pleasing to be regarded as scholarly if not as scholars. Their choice of specialized methods applied to the all-inclusive past propels them further along the way so that a harmonizing of interests seems imminent. My present concern, however, is not to scrutinize this process but to consider the values in individual programs that might prove useful in a synthesis.

Quite aware that he must work in defiance of criticism's ukase against biography, Leon Edel has become the champion of the "art of literary biography," an art which should involve a complete critical knowledge of the works of the author. Unlike the biographer of Chaucer or Shakespeare, the modern literary biographer is all but overwhelmed by his materials. "How different," Mr. Edel remarks enviously, "is the task of the critic, especially the 'new critic'! His table, in contrast to the biographer's, is uncluttered. No birth certificates, no deeds, no letters, no diaries, no excess literary baggage: only the works, to be read and re-read, pondered and analysed. . . . The literary biographer, however, must at every moment of his task be a critic. His is an act of continual and unceasing criticism." All of us who have read the first three volumes of Edel's unfinished life of Henry James realize how much he has done to restore biography to an acceptable literary standard for both criticism and scholarship, despite the fact that Henry James himself had taken many steps to defeat him, declaring at twenty-nine, before he had written his first novel, "artists, as time goes on will be likely to take alarm, empty their table-drawers and level the approaches to their privacy. The critics, psychologists and gossip mongers may then glean amid the stubble." The life of Henry James is no pinwheel accomplishment, like Strachey's *Eminent Victorians* or Thomas Beer's *Stephen Crane*, but a substantial and enduring literary work.

Freudian literary criticism, a generic term for all types of analysis dealing with the creative psyche, has been one of the easiest methods for the former new critics to resort to, for it contains no inherent compulsion to abandon the text. Freud himself, equipped with a considerable knowledge of literature and a keen sensibility, provided models for this kind of criticism. In *The Interpretation of Dreams*, for example, he suggested that Hamlet's unconscious guilt arising from his own Oedipal desires inhibited Hamlet from avenging his father. "Hamlet is able to do anything but take vengeance upon the man who did away with his father and has taken his father's place with his mother— the man who shows him in realization the repressed desires of his own childhood. The loathing which should have driven him to revenge is thus repressed by conscientious scruples which tell him that he himself is no better than the murderer whom he is required to punish." Capricious and unorthodox, D. H. Lawrence employs his own version of the method with such startling skill at times that Edmund Wilson has declared *Studies in Classic American Literature* to be "one of the few first-rate books to have been written on the subject." Here is Lawrence's interpretation of the close of *The Scarlet Letter*: "Right to the end Dimmesdale must have his saintly triumphs. He must preach his Election Sermon, and win his last saintly applause. At the same time he has an almost imbecile, epileptic impulse to defile the religious reality he exists in.

In Dimmesdale at this time lies the whole clue to Dostoevsky."

It is no response to the Freudian critic to say that an author's intention was something other than the critic's interpretation, for the Freudian critic may know the author's motivation better than the author himself; indeed, once literature is confined to the couch, the Freudian speaks with an authority no other critic can assume. Yet a suspicion lingers that Mr. Leslie Fiedler is not always right when he assumes that every pure maiden in American fiction is but a cover for the author's animosity toward all women, and with difficulty we repress the cry, "Physician, heal thyself." Leon Edel properly cautions the Freudian to examine his grounds of attraction to, or repulsion from, an author as a basis for determining his critical stances, and this appears to be the area of real vulnerability for the Freudian. If I may tease my truly distinguished colleague, I might observe that he has sometimes appeared to feel that he might have made a better brother, in a situation of sibling rivalry, to Henry James than did William. It is a curious fact that both Henry and his biographer have philosopher brothers. That the subconscious mind of an artist is the reservoir of his invention is generally conceded. The "infamous insurance scheme" which constitutes the plot of The Wings of the Dove I find exists in a French novel that James had read thirty-five years earlier and possibly had forgotten. Who can say, however, that a process of gestation was not going on in his subconscious mind?

Plot parallels suggest not merely an immediate borrowing from a literary predecessor but the possibility of a remote prototype or common ancestor for similar works. This idea is basic to Sir James Frazer's great work, The Golden Bough, in which this Scottish anthropologist traced numerous myths back to their prehistoric and ritualistic beginnings. Carl Jung's theory that the subconscious of man is a storehouse of racial, as well as personal, history reinforced the importance of myth in creative life, and T. S. Eliot's confession that Miss Jessie Weston's

From Ritual to Romance had influenced the creation of *The Waste Land* pointed out to the new critics a path for exploration when they found *explication de texte* too narrow a ground. Although certain British critics—F. M. Cornford, Jane Harrison, Gilbert Murray, and Andrew Lang—had dealt previously with the ritualistic background of Greek myths, it is Maud Bodkin in *Archetypal Patterns in Modern Poetry* who introduces the methods of Frazer and Jung into the study of modern literature and provides models for others to follow. Hamlet, the prime anatomical target for critical surgery in the last three hundred years, is astonishingly carved and served by Miss Bodkin. Probing the wound opened by Freud and enlarged by Ernest Jones, she accepts Hamlet as the victim of an Oedipal situation, but both Claudius and the elder Hamlet are components of the "father image," thus setting up a conflict, or "inner tension," which can only be relieved by the death of the tragic hero. The hero develops toward himself an ambivalent attitude resulting in an ego desiring self-assertion and an ego craving surrender to a greater power than itself, "the community consciousness." Thus the death of Hamlet becomes a submission or sacrifice to the tribe, like the ritual sacrifice of a king or sacred animal for the renewal of the life of the tribe. This is the significance of Hamlet's final charge to Horatio to "draw thy breath in pain, / To tell my story." Now, I find this ingenious and even fascinating, but I wonder if it is criticism. If all the great literature of the world can be reduced to a few mythological rites or archetypal patterns, do not the distinctions between works, as Professor Meyer H. Abrams contends, become less and less, and vanish? Archetypal criticism, even though it satisfies Mr. Eliot's criterion of elucidation, moves steadily away from works of art (the area of criticism) to folk superstitions (the area of the anthropologist and folklorist).

Yet if tribal rites, which symbolize elemental social processes, can be shown as buried in the racial subconscious and related in even the vaguest way to the creative psyche, why does not this fact validate the use the writer makes of his economic and social background as a means of evaluating him? Surely as much of the creative act is conscious as unconscious. Surely modern society has as many rituals of which the artist is aware as tribal rites of which he is unconscious but by which he is influenced. Mr. Eliot did not get his contempt for the Jew, the Irish, and the Cockney out of Miss Weston's book, but out of his experience, out of his connection with Lloyd's bank, his reaction to the Irish rebellion, his acquaintance with London pubs, and out of the vulgar stereotypes of his society. How is one to elucidate or scrutinize Steinbeck's *The Grapes of Wrath* with no reference to the Dust Bowl, the tractoring out of the Okies, or the labor practices of the farmers' association of California? Yet it was fully as much against sociological criticism as biographical criticism that the new criticism rebelled. Such books as Edmund Wilson's *To the Finland Station* or Granville Hicks's *The Great Tradition* seem, in retrospect, more in the nature of political tracts than works of criticism. They were, however, phenomena of the depression, and Wilson and Hicks, as well as Lionel Trilling, employing the social background of writers whom they examine, without a political *parti pris*, seem to me as able critics as America possesses. Irving Howe and Norman Podhoritz, also, with this approach, have on occasion written analyses of high merit. The lesson learned is that, while a writer's social views affect his judgment and may properly be remarked and weighed, we must ever—and without ambivalence— keep his work as an artist to the fore.

Mere elucidation must have appeared in this discussion increasingly inadequate as a definition of the function of criticism. While sticking to his contention that "poetry is not the inculcation of morals, or the direction of politics," Eliot admitted, in his Preface to the second edition of *The Sacred Wood*, that poetry did have "something to do with morals, and with religion, and even with politics," though he could not say what. Less hesitant than he, a group of writers, of whom Mr. Ivor Winters is the best known, have emphasized a moral approach to literature. In an essay called "Robert Frost, or the Spiritual Drifter as Poet"

Winters declares, as a result of examining four carefully selected poems, to which "The Road Not Taken" is the key, that Frost has neither "the intelligence or energy to become a major poet." The substance of the poem is very familiar: facing the choice of divergent roads in a wood, Frost chose the least traveled one and declares his choice has "made all the difference." Winters concedes that the poet has described a comprehensible predicament—"his poem is good as far as it goes, [but] . . . it does not go far enough, it is incomplete, and it puts on the reader a burden of critical intelligence which ought to be borne by the poet." This is a just stricture, so far as this particular poem is concerned, and more or less just in regard to the companion pieces. But the selective process through which Winters condemns Frost has been somehow characteristic of moral criticism: the human limitation, whatever it is, looms larger than the general conduct of the man. Frost is no spiritual drifter in "The Black Cottage," "New Hampshire," "To a Thinker," or dozens of other poems. If "poetry is the record of the best and happiest moments," as Shelley thought, "of the best and happiest minds," it is essentially ethical, for who can imagine a superior mind finding delight in the discomfort of others? Since literature ceased providing, in the early years of our century, examples of superior conduct, as in Tom Tulliver, Henry Esmond, Captain McWhirr, and Max Gottlieb, and confined itself to the lot of the underprivileged and the outcast, its motivation has been empathy. Empathy by its very nature is ethical—it assumes redemptive power in a situation. The business of the critic is then, so far as it is ethical, to determine the quality of the empathy. Is it bathetic? Is it directed toward worthless objects? Does the author lower himself or degrade society to raise his object? So many of the answers lie in psychology and sociology that a critic, giving appreciative attention, needs to be very sure of his training before he does so; nevertheless, this is an area for fair employment of his sensibilities, and at the moment his emphasis in criticism is most needed and rarest.

The chief defect, however, of an approach to literature

through only one method is the presumption that, if pursued with the utmost efficiency, it should extract all the values of a work of art. Yet if art in any sense mirrors life, it mirrors a complexity unyielding to a monist approach. I cannot go so far as Mr. Eliot and assert a poem means whatever it means to a reader, for this might reduce it to having no meaning at all, but I am willing to concede to a masterpiece many powers of ever renewing the delight it gives. Ours is a pluralistic universe, to borrow a phrase from William James, a universe without stability, its order ever threatened by disorder, a universe of contingency and change. In so far as the work of art mirrors that universe it must partake somewhat of its pluralism, even of its transiency. "Values are as unstable as the forms of clouds," John Dewey tells us. "Cultivated taste alone is capable of prolonged appreciation of the same object; and it is capable of it because it has been trained to a discriminating procedure which constantly uncovers in the object new meanings to be perceived and enjoyed." Forgotten and recovered meanings are also capable of producing delight. The instability of the very language in which a poem is written is at once a defect and a virtue: original meanings decay but the language takes on new meanings conveying new pleasures. Yet as compared with life itself, it has a relative kind of transient fixity, a retarded instability of meaning. These are the qualities that attract the reader away from the uncertainty of life to art. It is the relative "permanence" of art that solicits continuous attention fully as much as its other values. The obligation of the critic is to approach the work of art with every faculty, with every technique, with every method he can command, for he must know not only what the poem probably meant to its creator but also what it probably means to several different kinds of readers in his own generation if he is to communicate his appreciation and delight to them. In a word, he must have the keenest sense of time to deal with the pluralistic values of any given work of art; he must himself be a pluralist, athletically able to keep receding values in view, willing to embrace new values as they come on, in order to dispense in acceptable language an appreciation appropriate to the sensibilities of the youngest of his generation as the purest form of judgment. His role, if properly understood, is neither that of ambassador of the old nor ambassador of the new, for each is a partisan, but of liaison officer between the two. It is the role of both scholar and critic.

AFTERWORD

One special merit of using several critical methods in examining a work of art is the confirmation they should supply each other. Too many authors have confessed that they no longer know what they meant or intended for one to consider the author's meaning, hitherto so often the aim of criticism, as the goal of interpretation. Nor is it quite proper to assert that a poem means "whatever it means to you." This is to surrender to a subjective impressionism. Neither should one be satisfied with what might be termed "gross meaning," which is the sum of the subjective impressionisms of any selected moment. Gross meaning is what we probably arrive at when we try to state the meaning of *Hamlet* from a study of Shakespeare's life, backgrounds, language, and other plays by himself, his predecessors, and his contemporaries. This merely produces what he *might* have meant under these limitations, what Shakespeare's audience might have understood him to mean. Beneath it lies an "intrinsic meaning" which never certainly can be got at. The aim of the critic should be a "viable meaning," that is, a meaning acceptable, with all its conceivable values, to the best sensibilities of the critic's time and place. This is what the best critics of Shakespeare arrive at in their circumstances, which are neither those of Shakespeare nor tomorrow's circumstances. I should not have trusted my reader to infer this. Its omission is the essay's chief defect.

This essay was originally presented as the Founders Day address at New York University on April 23, 1964, an occasion for the assembly of honors students in the different schools of the University and for honoring a selected three of the faculty for distinguished teaching. It was first printed by the University. Only one or two local allusions have been stricken and a few pleasantries permitted the speaker on such an occasion.

2 WALT WHITMAN AND HIS
LEAVES OF GRASS

THIS IS ONE of the world's great books. Unique in form, charged persuasively with feeling, at once coarse and delicate in texture, *Leaves of Grass* owes its eminence not to one of these qualities especially, nor even to their assemblage, but rather to the fact that it concentrates in its pages the native wit and wisdom of a people when that wit and wisdom was still strongly colored by animal faith and was as yet uncorroded by the vinegar of suspicion, the subtle acid of doubt, the harsh caustic of fear.

"It is a great thing for a Nation," wrote Thomas Carlyle, "that it get an articulate voice; that it produce a man who will speak-forth what the heart of it means!" The articulate voice of a nation is not the echo of a coterie, of a class, or of a section; it is the murmur and cadence of the whole mass shaped into utterance, it is the dumb wonder of the dead average made expressive, it is the medley of the multitude brought into time and tune. To blend into a common rhythm the systole and diastole of many million hearts, to pick the central thread of meaning from the skein tangled by the crowd, requires seer and prophet, or even genius, in the rare or tutelary sense. When the Yea-Sayer arrives who does this, the event seemingly is not of a mundane order but approximates the supernatural; hence the tutelary spirit is taken for a fraud or an impostor, "a fool or a churl," for a long time. How singular the event that the right man should be present with ear to catch the pulse of the people is evidenced by the fact that, though we have given them our suffrage, few of our Presidents would satisfy us at once as the guiding genius, the representative man, or even the voice of an era. A deeper sympathy, a broader comprehension, a closer proximity to the core make Whitman the chosen one. It is because *Leaves of Grass*, like the *Divine Comedy* or *Don Quixote*, is the product of a time-selected man that it is one of the world's great books.

Nostalgically looking backwards from our age of anxiety, another American poet has said that "America was promises." Hope was at its highest level in this country in the great period of literary fruitage between Emerson's *The American Scholar* in 1837 and *Leaves of Grass* in 1855. Many then tried to express the spirit of that Golden Day and gave us handsome and enduring books, but Whitman alone breathed its total essence. Glancing, they apprehended a fraction, whereas he with steadfast scrutiny took in the sum of things and their meaning. They checked not at noon what they had received in the bright morning of their perceptions; Whitman at nightfall was still engaged with his vision. *Leaves of Grass* is America's most revised book. It was revised meaningfully seven times in twenty-six years; nevertheless it remained essentially the same book, for the effort was ever to state more forcefully, more persuasively, the original message of hope. Whitman kept his faith—he did not sink into the slough of despond in which most intellectuals lose themselves and dignity as they age. Admirable was the determination that made the poet persist in perfecting his book, and in the process poetry became prophecy, a standard and measure for what is best in the American experiment. It is in this sense that *Leaves of Grass* is a tutelary book, the product of genius. And its maker is an exemplary creator: more than the representative man of his age, he is the poet-prophet of the bardic tradition—the representative man in poetry for his country.

In the circumstances of Whitman's birth, childhood, and young manhood there is less than no hint of his future greatness. Born on May 31, 1819, in Huntington Township, on Long Island, New York, Walt Whitman was the product of a union of families without distinction. The father, for whom the poet was named, was a carpenter by trade. A morose man, by all accounts, and uncompanionable, he does not appear to have been very close to any of his children, and probably least of all to his namesake, who was his wife's favorite. Of him the poet has left a sharp vignette:

> The father, strong, self-sufficient, manly, mean, angered, unjust.
> The blow, the quick loud word, the tight bargain, the crafty lure. . . .

Walt's great attachment to his mother, who was Louisa Van Velsor before her marriage, induced him to leave reverential portraits of her, misleading to his biographers, for she seems to have been ignorant, vulgar, and self-centered. A fat bundle of common ills, she later pled poverty with money in the bank and, snuffling, made her letters to Walt long rehearsals of her miseries. The poet, excessively tolerant of her faults, echoed her bad grammar and puerile style in correspondence with her to avoid even the implication of criticism. Such a picture of her as he gave John Burroughs led the latter to conclude, "From the immediate mother of the poet come, I think, his chief traits."

One sees, perhaps, as many of them in her other children, who were, on the whole, a sorry brood. Jesse, a little over a year older than Walt, after following the sea, ended his days in a lunatic asylum in 1870. Though his insanity was attributed to a fall from a mast and also to a beating by thugs, it is a good guess that a congenital weakness was responsible. As with the oldest Whitman boy, so with the youngest: Edward, born in 1835, was a feeble-minded epileptic, with a crippled arm and leg. Six years Walt's junior, Andrew Whitman succumbed in his thirties to what was accepted as tuberculosis of the throat; his widow, who was looked upon by Mrs. Whitman as a slut, was charged with streetwalking. An unnamed infant, born before Andrew, died at six months. If not mad herself, Walt's sister Hannah tortured her husband, a French landscape painter by the name of Charles L. Heyde, into madness. Always depicting herself as abused, Hannah was an incompetent housekeeper and an escapist to whom frequent illness was a refuge; her physician declared her disease "irremedial by medicine." One can hardly conjecture what these people were like as children and associates of the future poet. But there were also Mary Elizabeth, a sister two years younger, and two other brothers, Thomas Jefferson (called "Jeff" in the family) and George, who do not seem to have been affected by the father's instability or the mother's physical flabbiness. Mary later married a shipbuilder and lived happily at Greenport, New York, where Walt sometimes visited her; Jeff, after working under Moses Lane, Chief Engineer of the Brooklyn Water Works, found a similar but more remunerative position in St. Louis, lived there comfortably, and made occasional contributions to the support of the indigent members of the family. George was the most competent of the Whitmans, aside from Walt. Getting a leg up by earning a commission in the Civil War, he later became a successful businessman. But these well members of the Whitman family exhibit no traits that one would expect to find in the blood kin of genius. Neither the sister nor either of the brothers was a book lover or even a reader. Possibly the poet could have been born into a home with fewer advantages, but it is hard to think what else it might have lacked.

That home was moved about frequently in Whitman's youth. When he was "still in frocks," the family left the West Hills farmhouse, in Huntington, for a place on Front Street, near the ferry slip, in Brooklyn, but in the next four years it occupied as many residences, two of which the elder Whitman built himself but lost in foreclosures. At six Walt began his education in the public schools; he impressed his teacher, Benjamin Halleck, only with his "good nature, his clumsiness, and his poverty of special promise." Two recollections of his childhood were ever vivid to Whitman: he remembered the benevolence of Lafayette, who, attending the Independence Day ceremonies in 1825, had promiscuously kissed him as one of the children in the crowd; and he remembered the impassioned eloquence of Elias Hicks, the Quaker preacher, whom he was taken to hear by his father and mother as a reward for "behaving well that day."

Whitman got his first employment when he was either ten or eleven years old and probably quit school at about the same time. He was first an office boy for a lawyer and then for a doctor. In 1831 he was introduced to a print shop as an errand boy and eventually he became a 'prentice printer and then a full-fledged compositor on the Long Island *Star*, a position he held from the autumn of 1832 until May, 1835. Meanwhile his family had moved back into the country because Mrs. Whitman was ill, and Whitman, after setting type for another year in New York City, decided to follow them.

Whitman's work as a compositor had made him a "knowledgeable" young man, and he sufficiently impressed the school boards in successive impoverished districts so that he was permitted to embark upon a "profession"— that of teaching. Between 1836 and 1838 he taught short terms in Norwich, in "the school west of Babylon," in Long Swamp, and in Smithtown. In the last place he helped to revive the debating society and served as its secretary. In the records which he kept (and which still survive) is the first evidence of a mind awakened to contemporary issues, for the society chose current topics and Whitman, loser in the earlier debates, was a fairly consistent winner later, showing that he acquired skill and substance.

Having left Smithtown, he got backing to issue a weekly newspaper at Huntington, the *Long Islander*, which first appeared on June 5, 1838. Less than a year later he was removed as editor by his backers who allegedly were displeased with the irregular appearance of the paper. Whitman taught school again, and in the latter part of 1839 returned to his trade as typesetter, working for James

L. Brenton, owner of the *Long Island Democrat*, in Jamaica. This connection, though brief, was important, for, like many printers before him, Whitman turned author and contributed prose and verse to the *Democrat*. Conventional and sentimental, these pieces have slight merit, though their prevailing liberalism and humanitarianism should be noted. The campaign of 1840 drew Whitman into politics and he electioneered for Martin Van Buren. Returning to New York City after five busy years on Long Island, Whitman first worked as compositor for the *New York World*, after which he was, in quick succession, editor of the *Aurora*, the *Tatler*, the *Statesman*, and the *New York Democrat*. The proprietor of the first of these journals did not care for him and pronounced him "the laziest fellow who ever undertook to edit a city paper." He was only twenty-three, and perhaps the responsibility was too much for him; a photograph taken a little earlier shows him affecting the dress of a dandy and he may for the moment have been too conscious of his rise in the world.

If Whitman neglected his editorial responsibilities, he can hardly be termed lazy, for he was very busy with his pen, contributing to such reputable periodicals as the *Democratic Review*, the *Broadway Journal*, the *American Review*, and the *Columbian Magazine*. On the score of artistry, he hardly provided models for the other contributors, yet he appears to have made out as a free-lancer with this work. The year 1842 saw the appearance of his first book, a temperance novel entitled *Franklin Evans*. Later, when Whitman was adopted by the Bohemian element, he repudiated this book, declaring he had written it in the reading room of Tammany Hall after fortifying himself at a neighboring bar with gin cocktails. Nevertheless the book probably accurately represents an early conviction for temperance. Describing the perfect father in the "Children of Adam" section of *Leaves of Grass*, Whitman wrote, "He drank water only, the blood show'd like scarlet through the clear-brown skin of his face." And again, enumerating the ideal companions, both in "Song of the

Open Road" and in "Pioneers, O Pioneers," Whitman
excluded the "rum-drinker" and the "diseas'd person." It is
likely that Jesse Whitman, later a drunkard, was already
indulging too much, but if that were not so, Whitman was
enough of the young crusader, as his position on corporal
punishment in the schoolroom, on capital punishment for
crime, and on slavery reveals, for him to have adopted
abstinence as an issue.

More attentive once again to writing than to his editing,
and in consequence losing a number of jobs, Whitman
nevertheless secured, in 1846, the relatively important post
of editor of the *Brooklyn Daily Eagle*. In January, 1848, he
either resigned or was discharged from this position
because of his sharp difference in politics with Isaac Van
Anden, the owner. Both Van Anden and Whitman were
Democrats, but the former was a stand-pat regular or
"Hunker," whereas Whitman, a "Barnburner," was critical of the party for its failure to support the Wilmot
Proviso and free soil. At any rate, Whitman's connection
with the *Eagle* was terminated after he had chastised
General Lewis Cass editorially on January 3 for attacking
the Proviso.

Shortly after this episode Whitman was invited by the
founder to go to New Orleans to help edit a new paper
there called the *Crescent*. On February 11 he left Brooklyn
with his brother Jeff, and after traveling by stage and boat,
arrived in Louisiana about two weeks later. A part of his
trip he celebrated in a conventional poem, entitled "Sail-
ing the Mississippi at Midnight," in the first issue of the
Crescent on March 5, 1848. Walt worked for his new
owner only a little over two months, resigning on May 24.
It has been assumed that negligence of his editorial duties
may have led to his severance from the *Crescent*, yet other
factors seem to have operated, too. Jeff was homesick and
ill, and it is hard to believe that an ardent Barnburner
could have existed in New Orleans without feeling hamstrung. It should be noted that, after his return to
Brooklyn on June 15, he was hailed as a champion
returned to the lists, and that, in September, he became

editor of the *Brooklyn Freeman*, founded to advance the "Free Soil" campaign of that year, in which Whitman actively participated. When the Free Soilers returned to the ranks of the Democratic Party, Whitman resigned his editorship (September 11, 1849), even though he had transformed the *Freeman* from a weekly to a successful daily. The evidence would seem to indicate that it was politics in part which drew Whitman back North.

Whitman's New Orleans trip has interested biographers for yet another reason. On August 19, 1890, Whitman wrote J. A. Symonds, an English devotee, "My life, young manhood, mid-age, times South, Etc., have been jolly, bodily, and doubtless open to criticism. Though unmarried I have had six children—two are dead—one living Southern grandchild, fine boy, writes to me occasionally—circumstances (connected with their fortune and benefit) have separated me from intimate relations." Horace Traubel, who aspired to be Walt's Boswell, cognizant of this "confession," relates that Whitman saw one of his "grandchildren" on a day that Traubel was denied the master's presence and hazarded the conjecture that the child was black. Hence arose the hypothesis of an octoroon or Creole mistress in New Orleans. But it is very important to note that Whitman's "confession" was elicited by a query from Symonds as to whether or not the seemingly homosexual poems of the "Calamus" section reveal a personal aberration. This shocked Whitman who hotly denied the implication and added the "confession." It is possible, then, that Whitman hastily invented his illicit amorous career to confound whoever, like Symonds, might try to read the "Calamus" poems as subjective revelation. His behavior seemingly was parallel when he was taxed with teetotalism. So far as Whitman's biographers are aware, there is only one piece of evidence beyond the "confession" to support the contention that Whitman ever had an affair with a woman. There exists a self-admonitory note, dated July 15, 1870, in which he apparently counsels himself to break off a relationship that can come to nothing:

TO GIVE UP ABSOLUTELY & *for good,* from *this present hour,* this FEVERISH, FLUCTUATING, *useless undignified pursuit of* 164—*too long,* (*much too long*) persevered in,—so humiliating—*It must come at last* & had better come now—(*It cannot possibly be a success*) LET THERE BE FROM THIS HOUR NO FALTERING, NO GETTING—at all henceforth, (NOT ONCE, *under any circumstances*)—*avoid seeing her, or meeting her, or any talk or explanations*—or ANY MEETING WHAT-EVER, *FROM THIS HOUR FORTH, FOR LIFE.*

The usual interpretation of this passage is that Whitman may have become infatuated with a married woman in Washington. Peter Doyle, a young streetcar conductor with whom Whitman is sometimes accused of having had unnatural relations and with whom he was extremely familiar, has said, however, "I never knew a case of Walt's being bothered up by a woman. Woman in that sense never entered his head. Walt was too clean. No trace of any kind of dissipation in him. I ought to know about him those years—we were awfully close together." Yet it is more than "bothersome" that if the number "164," under which Whitman disguised the name of the loved one, is broken into the component parts "16" and "4" and these are presumed to be numerically in the alphabet the initials of a person, they are those of Peter Doyle.

The period immediately after Whitman's return from the South and resignation from the *Freeman* is the period of the gestation of *Leaves of Grass.* Part of this time he lived alone and part of it with his family, first in a place on Myrtle Avenue, where he also had a bookstore, and then at other locations. "We were all at work—all except Walt," his brother George remembered. The poet, he said, "wrote a little, worked a little, loafed a little," despite which "he made a living now." Whitman's father and his brothers (all trained to carpentry) made money during the Brooklyn building boom, so graphically described in "Song of the Broad-Axe." And so did Walt. He records that he built and sold several houses, naming their location. And it has recently been revealed that he hired out by the day. He continued to do some free-lance work, contributing to the *Brooklyn Daily Advertiser* and the *New York Evening Post*. Yet his preoccupation was with his creative work. On March 22, 1850, he published in Greeley's *Tribune* his first free verse poem, a rebuke to Webster for supporting the Fugitive Slave Law, entitled "Blood Money." But he was not yet certain that poetry was his true bent: on scraps of paper he set down ideas which could be the germs of either poems or lectures. "I guess it was in those years," his brother George remembered, "he had an idea he could lecture. He wrote what mother called 'barrels' of lectures." But suddenly things were clarified for him and *Leaves of Grass* was the result. It was issued on July 4, 1855, with the author himself as publisher. Whitman had set the type with his own hands at the print shop of Andrew and James Rome, two of his friends.

A flattering letter from Emerson and some adroit promotion on Whitman's part (which included writing anonymous reviews of himself) did more than sell the book—it created a demand for it. There was a second edition in 1856 and a third in 1860. Meanwhile Whitman, variously engaged in journalism, had altered the course of his life. Prior to 1855 he had assumed the clothing of a laboring man or carpenter and had begun to cultivate the company of bus drivers and ferrymen. Moncure Conway, who visited him in September, 1855, at Emerson's suggestion, tells how he walked with him and how Whitman was " 'hail fellow' with every man he met, all apparently in the laboring class. He says he is one of that class by choice; that he is personally dear to some thousands of such in New York, who 'love him but cannot make head or tail of his book.' "

One of the strongest grounds of the affection in which Whitman was held by the working man was his service to the ill and destitute in the hospitals of Brooklyn and New York, which began at this time. In the first year of the Civil War wounded soldiers found their way into these hospitals and were nursed by Whitman. News coming in December, 1862, that his brother George, a volunteer, had been injured, Walt departed for the front in Virginia. Discovering that George had a mere scratch and that the inadequate hospitals in Washington were crowded with badly wounded men in dire need of attention, Whitman stayed on as a self-appointed "missionary" and nurse. Out of solicited contributions and out of his small earnings in the office of a paymaster of the army, he purchased medicines and comforts for the men; he wrote letters for them to their relatives on request and soothed them when they were delirious. In poor health, he gave of himself unstintingly and won the lasting gratitude of the veterans. After his death, Dr. Richard M. Bucke brought together Whitman's letters and a few of the newspaper articles he had written on the condition of the men and published them under the title *The Wound-Dresser* (1898). Second only to *Leaves of Grass*, this is his finest book. In it an heroic man has recorded with simple feeling the heroic sufferings of others, the soldiers of the North and the South.

After he had in a measure recuperated from his tremendous fatigue, Whitman assumed a clerkship in the Indian Bureau, in the Department of the Interior, on January 24, 1865. Six months later, on June 30, despite an interim promotion, he was dismissed by Secretary James Harlan. Whitman's version of this episode is that Harlan, going through his desk after hours, came upon a copy of *Leaves of Grass* and discharged the poet as the author of "an indecent book." Whitman's many friends interceded for him and a month later he was given another clerkship, this time in the Attorney General's Office. In September, William O'Connor, a Washington newspaperman and an old friend, wrote an indignant book defending Whitman from the Harlan charges. *The Good Gray Poet*, published under O'Connor's name, may possibly have been either supervised, emended, or partially written by the poet himself, for it has the earmarks of his prose style; but *Notes on Walt Whitman as Poet and Person* (1867), though it bore as its author the name of John Burroughs, another friend, was largely composed by Whitman himself. Whatever these books did to establish his fame was surpassed when the English literati adopted him, following the publication of a bowdlerized edition of his poetry in that country which Whitman permitted William Rossetti to make in 1868. Swinburne hailed him in *Songs Before Sunrise* (1872) and Tennyson wrote to express appreciation of his verse. In a bold move, Dartmouth College invited him to read a poem of his composing at its 1872 commencement. Though ridicule and abuse outweighed praise during the rest of his life, he was on the way now to acceptance.

In the post–Civil War years, the most notable things to come from his pen were *Drum Taps* (1865), containing in all but a few copies "When Lilacs Last in the Dooryard Bloom'd," by common consent his greatest single poem; *Democratic Vistas* (1871), a prose volume, in which, while admitting that moral turpitude was prevalent in the republic, Whitman reaffirmed his faith in the grand conglomerate of the people; and "A Backward Glance O'er Travel'd Roads," an important summary view of his poetic career, which was first published in an incomplete form in the English edition of *Democratic Vistas* (1888). He also put in shape his *Complete Prose Works* (1892), which contains, among other things, the autobiographical "Specimen Days."

On January 23, 1873, Whitman suffered an incapacitating attack of paralysis. This affliction had caused the death of his father a week after *Leaves of Grass* was published and was to cause the death of his sister Mary. Whitman's descriptions of himself and his account of his various struggles with his health, both during the Civil War and after, suggest that he was a victim of high blood pressure, a condition leading to paralysis. What he believed to have been a sunstroke early in his career was probably the first manifestation of his affliction. In view of his condition, his fulsome giving of himself in the hospital wards during the war was rash in the extreme. Nursing for him was not merely the distribution of dainties or of assurances; it meant emotional involvement also. "I feel well and hearty enough," he writes, "but my feelings are kept in a painful condition a great part of the time." There are reports in his letters of spells of dizziness. "I had spells of deathly faintness and bad trouble in my head, too. . . . The doctors say it will pass over—*they have long told me I was going in too strong*." Prostration inevitably followed, yet after recuperating and returning to Washington, Whitman kept up his visits to the hospitals until the paralytic stroke of 1873. For his clerkship he hired a substitute, but the job was taken away from him in June, 1874, when it was clear that he would not be able to return to it. Meanwhile he had gone to live with his brother George in Camden, New Jersey. Here, and at Stafford Farm, at Timber Creek, he achieved the semblance of health. But it was certain that he could not be very active again. Leisurely visits to friends and relatives and occasional public appearances were the sum of his physical activities. If "The Prayer of Columbus" was written before his stroke, he composed no great poetry after that event. The success of the 1881 edition made it possible for him to buy a small house on Mickle Street, Camden, and cease to be a burden to his brother. When sales of his works fell off, friends helped with contributions and public benefits. In 1885 he had a second "sunstroke"; in 1888, another attack of paralysis brought him near to death. Whitman died at his home, on March 26, 1892, from the "indirect effects" of paralysis, according to Richard M. Bucke, his biographer, who was also a physician.

"Poems distilled from other poems will probably pass away," Whitman wrote in the Introduction to the first edition of *Leaves of Grass* in 1855. "Remember the book arose," he cautioned Dr. Bucke, "out of my life in Brooklyn and New York from 1838 to 1853, absorbing a million people, with an intimacy, an eagerness, an abandon, probably never equalled." If Whitman is to be taken even partially at his word, his derivation should be sought in popular, rather than in literary or philosophical, origins. On the other hand, he freely admitted to John Townsend

Trowbridge that, had he not read Emerson "at the right moment" in 1854, *Leaves of Grass* might not have appeared the next year. "I was simmering, simmering, simmering; Emerson brought me to a boil." If Whitman seems to have appeared in response to Emerson's demand for his kind of creator in "The Poet," it is impossible to place Whitman historically where he belongs in the history of verse—at the terminal morain of the revolt against the closed couplet and neoclassicism—without naming Emerson. It is the latter with his irregular verse and indifference to rime (he called Poe "the jingle man") who links Whitman to Coleridge. But such a demonstration of position is wholly academic and no one would be more surprised by it than Whitman. As a writer of free verse he owed nothing to Emerson or Coleridge, though they *had* to precede him. Nor is it much more fruitful to point out that Blake, Tupper, Christopher Smart, and others had written verse somewhat like his before him.

Those critics who, having noted Whitman's fondness for the Italian opera, then enjoying a great vogue in New York, have also remarked the resemblance between his verses and those of the free translations of the librettos for the contemporary theatergoers, are the critics who have probably located the primary inspiration for Whitman's free verse. "But for the opera," Trowbridge also reports him as saying, "I could never have written *Leaves of Grass*." (This admission covers not only the versification but also the structure of many of his poems as well, wherein the devices of musical composition are imitated.) Whitman himself says, "I was fed and bred under the Italian dispensation, and absorb'd it, and doubtless show it." But having thus received his inspiration for free verse, he diligently made comparisons to perfect the form. It is not surprising to find him cautioning himself, "Don't fall into the Ossianic, *by any chance*." Nor to find that he carefully studied and adopted the ingenious parallelisms of Biblical verse. Nor to suppose that contemporary declamation taught him something. But the first impulse was popular.

As with versification, so with ideas. There are echoes of Emerson all through *Leaves of Grass.* "Consistency is the hobgoblin of little minds," said Emerson. Whitman wrote:

> *Do I contradict myself?*
> *Very well then I contradict myself,*
> *(I am large, I contain multitudes.)*

Emerson advised Man Thinking first of all to "Study Nature," and, as if in obedience to this injunction, Whitman symbolically studies a spear of grass to find out "what God and man is." But whereas Emerson's examination of Nature produced the assumption that "outward" reality exists merely for the "discipline" of the soul and is "mere phenomenon," Whitman's survey led him to the conclusion that what is termed Nature (and that importantly included the natural man) is quite as important as the soul. Supposing Emerson's books were to be absorbed by the republic, Whitman speculates, "what a well-washed and grammatical, but bloodless and helpless, race we should turn out!" To his friend, William Sloane Kennedy, the poet of *Leaves of Grass* maintained that the great difference between Emerson's work and his own is that "I found and find everything in the *common concrete,* the broadcast materials, the flesh, the common passions, the tangible and visible, etc., and *in the average,* and that I radiate, work from these outward—or rather hardly wish to leave here but to remain and celebrate it all. . . . *L. of G.'s* word *is the body, including all,* including intellect and soul; E.'s word is mind (or soul)."

It is for fear Kennedy or someone later will read into "I radiate, work from these outward" a metaphysical intent that Whitman clarifies by "I . . . hardly wish to leave here but to remain and celebrate it all." For Emerson, this life is the preparation, or discipline, for a Future Life; for Whitman, all that is consequential is the Here and the Now. In this sense *Leaves of Grass* is a critique of Transcendentalism, or as Emerson preferred to call it, Idealism. To suppose that Whitman framed this critique

out of the resources of his nature unassisted is to suppose
too much. Whitman and Emerson, to be sure, were the
very "antipodes" in temperament, but Whitman's critique
and his message were born from the ferment of low-
grade ideas set in motion by the new spirit, ideas appealing
to the popular intelligence rather than to the philosophical
mind. One of these was the idea of Perfectionism.
Essentially, the Perfectionist believed that perfection
belongs to this earth, is not the attribute of some vague,
ethereal existence. Whitman writes:

> In this broad earth of ours
> Amid the measureless grossness and the slag
>
> Enclosed and safe within its central heart
> Nestles the seed perfection.

And more boldly:

> And I will show you that there is no imperfection in the
>   present. . . .
> There was never any more inception than there is now,
> Nor any more youth nor age than there is now
> And will never be any more perfection than there is
>   now . . .

Whitman did not get his Perfectionism from Hegel, or
from Madame De Stael, or from Margaret Fuller, all of
whom it can be shown that he read, for it is not in them.
The Perfectionist cult seems to have been started by a
young Yale Divinity student by the name of John Humphrey Noyes as early as 1834, but it spread quickly and
soon had adherents in the metropolitan area, in Newark,
and in Philadelphia. Whitman may have picked Perfectionism up from any one of these sources, but it is most
likely that he got it from Noyes himself, who for several
years after 1848 was located at 41 Willow Place, Brooklyn,
as an active and prolific propagandist of the cult. Noyes,
believing that heaven could be established on this earth,
was attentive especially to the Biblical revelation of the
character of heaven. Discovering that there was "neither
giving nor having of marriage in heaven," Noyes advocated

communism in wives and founded several communities with that as one of his objects. He might well have imparted to Whitman some of his unorthodoxy in regard to the conventional view of love. The latter resolved that his poems should not celebrate "romantic" love, which had become a "stale" poetic theme. He proposed to celebrate and does celebrate "the dear love of comrades," the affection between man and man, which he thought could become a cement for institutions, for states, and even for nations.

To the "love of comrades," to fraternal love, he applies a discarded technical term "adhesiveness," which he took from the phrenologists, who opposed it to the term "amativeness," which they used for love between the sexes. Whitman was much influenced by the phrenologists, who then were enjoying a great vogue; indeed, the second edition of his book was issued by Fowler & Wells, the phrenological publishers—and one of his favorite ideas was that feeling or a state of health could be communicated by "animal magnetism," a kind of human electricity. He called his poems "health chants" and he promises, at the end of the "Song of Myself," to be "good health" to his reader, even after his death. Thus Whitman, who might seem to have something in common with Mary Baker Eddy, resembles her only because he drew ideas contemporaneously from a somewhat similar popular context. The noblest use that Whitman made of the idea of adhesiveness was in the Washington hospitals, where he gave of his own physical and psychical substance to refresh and to buoy up other men. Eventually he carried male love to such an extreme that he has been suspected of homosexuality. If expressing the passion involved him in unnatural practices, it would not appear that these endured for long. The most damaging bit of evidence is also evidence of his revulsion, if it can be taken for either. Whitman was not Oscar Wilde.

But one thing is very clear—so far as love is a primary theme of *Leaves of Grass*, and it is *the* primary theme—it is the love of his fellow man that Whitman celebrates. He did not get this idea from the phrenologists (Fowler, for example, is most conventional—see his *Sexual Science*) but from the contemporary revolt against romantic love, so widespread that even Emerson voices it in "All for Love." The "Children of Adam" section in *Leaves of Grass* is an afterthought (and written subsequent to Whitman's study of the realistic discussion of amativeness by the phrenologists; hence "feudal" or romantic love still does not appear in the *Leaves*), but the "Calamus" idea is there from the first.

In its best expression "the dear love of comrades" is the bond of union that Whitman felt between himself and every other man, however degraded. Whitman, for example, was no mere abolitionist: he identified himself with "the hounded slave" and felt on his own flesh the scourges. No person was too low for this identification, no person so contemptible that he could not be plucked up:

> *To the cotton-field drudge and cleaner of privies I lean,*
> *On his right cheek I put the family kiss,*
> *And in my soul I swear I will never deny him. . . .*
> *I seize the descending man and raise him with resistless*
>   *will,*
> *O despairer, here is my neck,*
> *By God, you shall not go down! hang your whole weight*
>   *upon me.*

Degenerates were not exempt from the identification, either, and with a rare compassion for his day Whitman included them in his company. An exalted sympathy, a sympathy that did not calculate the mathematics of "a man is known by the company he keeps," made Whitman a Christ-like figure to some of those who knew him, and has subjected him to ridicule. Nonetheless, he is in this our greatest democrat, the representative man of his age and our nation. The best lesson from Whitman is

> *Whoever walks a furlong without sympathy walks to his*
>   *own funeral drest in his shroud.*

AFTERWORD

One form of pluralistic criticism—and possibly the simplest—is to synthesize, so far as humanly possible, all of the previous important scholarship and criticism on the chosen topic while incorporating one's own observations. I believe that this essay on *Leaves of Grass* gathered all of the important facts about it and its author and all that was valued in each as of its date (1950). I was conscious that I owed information about the Whitman family to Katherine Molinoff, on his early creative efforts to Clifton Furness, on the origins of his verse form to Louise Pound, on his politics to Newton Arvin, on his nursing services to Charles Glicksberg. My general orientation I owed surely to a hundred, but especially to my friends Emory Holloway, Gay Wilson Allen, and Harold Blodgett. This acquaintance with what is best in what has been thought about an author disappeared so completely during the vogue of the New Criticism that one had the frequent impression that the practitioner one was reading was the first discoverer of the author. When working on my survey of the criticism and scholarship devoted to James's novels, this was borne in upon me many times, but no more forcefully than when I found an essay in one of our leading journals perfectly duplicating the commentary of one (with no suspicion of plagiarism) that had appeared thirty years earlier. My original contributions in this essay are the confirmation of a homosexual relation between Whitman and Peter Doyle, an evaluation of it, and the treatment of the Perfectionist theme. My reading of the Doyle-code allusion has since been confirmed by F. DeWolfe Miller's discovery in the MS of a period after 16 in the number 164. I regret not going more thoroughly into the mystique of Whitman's methods of healing by the transfer of his "electric" health.

3   THE MEDIEVALISM OF
      HENRY ADAMS

THE ARCHANGEL loved heights." Behind this audacious opening sentence of *Mont-Saint-Michel and Chartres* lurks the apologetic figure of Henry Adams in the guise of a charitable and much traveled "uncle" volunteering his services as guide to a kodak-snapping "niece" for a summer sojourn in France. Much significance may be harvested from this seriocomic contrast of the soaring angel on his lofty pedestal and the mouselike little man, pendant but dignified, accompanying some adopted Daisy Miller down the gangplank of an exhausted Cunarder at Cherbourg or Havre. Yet this significance must be gathered quickly, for a scudding cloud may obscure the Archangel and the seemingly substantial girl may melt into thin air, leaving us only the lonely globe-trotter and connoisseur of cathedrals—as enigmatical as ever.

Of the symbols—man and maid, and austere angel poised on the summit of the tower that crowns his church—the stone image is most easily guessed at. Indeed, Adams himself obligingly furnishes us an interpretation from the eleventh century:

> . . . The Archangel stands for Church and State, and both militant. He is the conqueror of Satan, the mightiest of all created spirits, the nearest to God. His place was where the danger was greatest; therefore you find him here. For the same reason he was, while the pagan danger lasted, the patron saint of France. So the Normans, when they were converted to Christianity, put themselves under his protec-

tion. . . . So soldiers, nobles, and monarchs went on pil-
grimage to his shrine; so the common people followed, and
still follow, like ourselves.

Yet what interest has the artless girl in this ancient
protector of the Normans? Has she not Adams? And why
the humility of her guide who could not, in all seriousness,
have thought of himself as one of "the common people"
and possibly would not have respected her as such? The
thought is almost obscene that he should bring her to
Mont-Saint-Michel merely to pamper her passing passion
for photography. Besides, the winged image of Saint
Michael is beyond the reach of the sharpest Graflex lens,
even in the possession of the most athletic American miss.
Perhaps he has chosen the Archangel merely as a text for a
vainglorious display of his learning—surely a temptation to
a former Harvard University professor and president of the
American Historical Association? Yet Adams is not exactly
in his dotage and is still possessed of wit enough to be
amused by our suggestion that both image and niece will
vanish precipitately with his first rolling period.

No, we must fetch our imaginations up to the style of
our author if we are to perceive the necessary connection of
things. In a word, we must start several hundred feet off
the ground and clear of all of the encumbrance of sober
facts to get anywhere at all with the symbolism. It is
breath-taking, but we are good for it, since reason tells us
that the empyrean should furnish the better view. Very
well then—the Archangel is not Saint Michael but Yggdra-
sill, Niece Daisy is not herself but the Little Lamb, and
Adams is plainly Ishmael. Further, these images have a
tendency to interfuse and mix.

i

When Henry Adams returned in 1868 from
London with his papa, who had been an extraordinarily
useful servant of the Republic at the Court of St. James
during our Civil War, he was a brilliant but spoiled boy.
To be sure, one does not gain this impression if one
confines his study of Adams to *The Education*, even

though one of the two chapters covering the interlude between the close of the War and the home-coming of Ambassador Charles Francis Adams is entitled "Dilettant-ism" and even though the author admits that he had "reached his twenty-seventh birthday without having advanced a step, that he could see, beyond his twenty-first." One comes away from *The Education* so infected with the author's pessimism that a conception of him as a light and purposeless fellow approaching thirty with no fixed career is all but impossible, despite the careless admissions of the author himself. That his chief anxiety in going to Washington was that the city "stood outside the social pale" is a sufficient indication that our knowledge of the elder Adams has engulfed our perception of the boy. We do better to thrust *The Education* into some dusty corner and forget it while we form our knowledge of Henry Adams on *The Letters* which Mr. Worthington Chauncey Ford has edited with discreet omissions. Instead of the acute analysis of British politics during the time when intervention in our War seemed imminent—an analysis which makes several chapters in *The Education* the liveliest sort of reading—*The Letters* show Henry merely to reflect his father's emotions and anxieties without and very sharp perception of what was going on. "I don't know what we are ever going to do with this damned old country," he wrote his brother Charles who was enduring a "long siege in mud and rain" in Virginia in 1863; "some day it will wake up and find itself at war with us, and then what a squealing there'll be. . . ." The same letter boasts that he has been "put up for a Club in St. James's Street, by Mr. Milnes"—a boast more revealing of his preoccupa-tions than his prior outburst of emotion against England. "The *Trent* affair . . . destroyed all our country visits," he had earlier complained to his soldier-brother. Subse-quent letters from London, in the year of Fredericksburg, Chancellorsville, Gettysburg, Vicksburg, and Chicka-mauga, show Henry Adams to be having "a very tolerable time" in the British capital though he feels "the want of that happy absurdity" he has enjoyed in American society.

"We are dragging our weary carcasses to balls and entertainments of every description," he sighs in a letter to Charles on June 25, 1863, and two weeks later, while "the rush and fuss of society is still going on," he gives his brother a more detailed account of his fearful regimen:

> One rides in the Park two hours in the morning, dines out in the evening, and goes to a ball; rises to a breakfast the next day; goes to a dance in the afternoon, and has a large dinner at home, from which he goes to another ball at half after eleven.

Despite the generous excisions of Mr. Ford, we may gather from the *Letters* that Henry Adams was not unsusceptible to feminine influence. On a sojourn in Italy in the April of Lincoln's assassination he was commissioned by Lady Frances Gordon to purchase for her "some stones of turquoise-blue." One letter to Charles Milnes Gaskell mentions Adams's discomfiture at Mrs. Story's, where he had attempted to introduce himself to "a pretty blonde in blue" only to find her a "monosyllabic Hebe" and closes with a request to Gaskell to tell a Miss Montgomery that "she looks like the Venus of Medici." Another missive to the same correspondent, after Adams's return to Portland Place, reveals that the author is regarded by his friend as shrewd enough to evaluate an object of the other sex: "By the way I did the Argyll girl, and rather liked her. She has a pretty complexion; and is very fresh and unaffected; at least, so I thought after ninety seconds conversation." Though "regularly done by those brutes of tailors," Adams is worried that too great attentiveness to a matron will make the young ladies think him a bore. At Baden-Baden, he finds the females "enough to make one's hair stand out in all directions." Cora Pearl, the notorious vampire, is there, and Adams readily adjusts his morals to the atmosphere of the resort, chiding Gaskell because the latter cannot "distinguish between *l'infidélité du corps et l'infidélité du cœur*." Back in London, Adams has the pleasure of taking a "lovely one," whom Gaskell had evidently marked as his own, to dinner, and he teases his friend by telling him "we were . . . somewhat gay. You can measure it by the fact that we became sentimental and poetical before we rose from table. I gave a short discursive sketch in about fifteen minutes, of the nature and objects of love. She blushed and listened. Of course I spoke only as your representative." Another dinner, out in Bayswater, at the home of an American girl who had married an Englishman, furnishes Adams with a happy release:

> . . . I admired her as a girl; she was fast but handsome and lively. I had a dinner there last night which carried me off my legs. I talked all the time, ate all the time, drank all the time. In short I was *en train*. I drank a great deal too much and fell desperately in love with my hostess and told her so. There are oases in the desert of life. Such a one was Inverness Terrace last night. . . .

Here, surely, was a lighter Adams than the whole chronicles of that illustrious family had hitherto provided. And here perhaps was an Adams who might have some difficulty in adjusting to the rougher exigencies of American life.

In the *Letters* there is no evidence to show that Henry Adams thought even once of a career for himself during all the while that he was assistant secretary to his father in London. He had apparently pinned his hopes on the expectation that in his father's political future—Charles Francis Adams was as likely a presidential possibility in 1868 as any one—lay ample provision for himself. Landing in July, Henry Adams spent a few weeks in Quincy and Boston, and then sought the solace of America's most fashionable resort:

> So far, life has been really pleasant. After finishing my article on Lyell which occupied me to the end of August, I went down to Newport which is a very gay sort of Torquay, and there I performed the butterfly with great applause, for a week. Everyone was cordial and the young women mostly smiled on me more beamingly than I had been accustomed to, during my residence among the frigid damsels of London.

In *The Education* Adams reports a bitter sense of being on the auction block with no bidders in sight, but the correspondence hardly shows him seriously troubled about his future. Again, looking backward to 1868, Adams remembered that he and his brother Charles had struck a bargain in Quincy for one to pursue the railroads and the other the press, in the hope that they would play into each other's hands; and that he had gone to Washington as affording the shortest path to New York journalism. The *Letters* do not reveal any such working harmony in the Adams family. In response evidently to an urgent letter from Charles to hurry up a political article, Henry asserts that he "may be a year or two in working it up," and, in point of fact, he never completed it. Four or five months later when Charles has charged him again with dilatoriness, Henry takes a high tone in his reply:

> . . . your ideas and mine don't agree, but they never have agreed. You like the strife of the world. I detest and despise it. You work for power. I work for my own satisfaction. You like roughness and strength; I like taste and dexterity. For God's sake, let us go our ways and not try to be like each other.

Most biographical sketches of Henry Adams imply that he acquitted himself well while in Washington from the middle of October 1868 till the beginning of October 1870. In those two years, however, his total output as a "journalist" was not over half a dozen articles, any one of which could have been put together in a week at the outside. "I dawdle here," Henry wrote in March 1869. "The life is pleasant, rather than otherwise, and I am more contented here than I could be elsewhere." The truth seems to be that the way of Henry in Washington is still the way of the dilettante. "Society accepts all sorts of impertinences from me, without showing its teeth," he could boast, like the Beau of Bath. His first "Session" paper in the *North American Review* provoked a response which must have hit pretty near home, judging from his past. This is his own account in an epistle to his English confidante, Gaskell:

> . . . I enclose to you a long slip from a Massachusetts

paper, probably the most widely circulated of all these Massachusetts papers, in which I am treated in a way that will, I think, delight you. Of course it is all nonsense. I am neither a journalist nor one of the three best dancers in Washington, nor have I a profound knowledge of the cotillion, though I confess to having danced it pretty actively. But you see I am posted as a sort of American Pelham or Vivian Gray. This amused me, but the part of the joke which pleased me less, was to come.

This leader was condensed into half a dozen lines by a western paper, and copied among the items of the column "personal" all over the country. In this form it came back to New York. Hitherto my skill as a dancer was kept a mere artistic touch to heighten the effect of my "brilliant" essay. Now however the paragraph is compressed to two lines. "H. B. A. is the author of article, etc., etc., etc. He is one of the three best dancers in W." The next step will be to drop the literary half, and preserve the last line, and I am in an agony of terror for fear of seeing myself posted bluntly: "H. B. A. is the best dancer in W." This would be fame with a vengeance.

The Pelham-Vivian Gray character is enlarged by other "confessions." In January 1870, Adams was supposed to be attentive to a young woman bringing a dowry of £200,000. In his eyes "her only attraction is that I can flirt with the poor girl in safety, as I firmly believe she is in a deep consumption and will die of it. I like peculiar amusements of all sorts, and there is certainly a delicious thrill, much in the manner of Alfred de Musset, in thus pushing one's amusements into the future world. . . . Is not this delightfully morbid?" With the coming of spring in 1870 he grew fatuous: "The young maidens no doubt adore me, but I am obdurate. . . . Have some one nice to flirt with me at Wenlock." Dining with "Jephtha's daughter" and muckraking Congress brought, however, their inevitable reward, and Henry Adams was properly scored on in a reply to his second "Session" article by a western senator in a phrase which he remembered for many a long day:

His article on the Session in the July *North American* had made a success. . . . It had been reprinted by the Democratic National Committee and circulated as a campaign document by the hundred thousand copies. . . . His only reward or return for this partisan service consisted in being formally answered by Senator Timothy Howe, of Wisconsin, in a Republican campaign document, presumably to be also freely circulated, in which the Senator, besides refuting his opinions, did him the honor—most unusual and picturesque in a Senator's rhetoric—of likening him to a begonia.

The begonia is, or then was, a plant of such senatorial qualities as to make the simile, in intention, most flattering. Far from charming in its refinement, the begonia is remarkable for curious and showy foliage; it was conspicuous; it seemed to have no useful purpose; and it insisted in standing always in the most prominent positions. Adams would have greatly liked to be a begonia in Washington, for this was rather his ideal of the successful statesman. . . .

In *The Education* the villain of Henry Adams's Washington career is President Grant. When Grant announced the make-up of his Cabinet in 1869, Adams knew that he himself had made "another inconceivable false start. . . . Grant had cut short the life which Adams had laid out for himself in the future. After such a miscarriage, no thought of effectual reform could revive for at least one generation, and he had no fancy for ineffectual politics." The General is roundly abused: Grant "had no right to exist. He should have been extinct for ages. . . . The progress of evolution from President Washington to President Grant, was alone evidence enough to upset Darwin." Yet the blunt-fingered General, conqueror of Lee, can hardly be said, even metaphorically, to have crushed the wings of this lovely butterfly. There is every indication that Adams's family came to the conclusion that his stay in Washington was utterly purposeless and made provision for him to leave. Indeed, in his disarming and invalidating fashion, Adams freely admits as much. While he was visiting at Wenlock Abbey in the summer of 1870, President Eliot had written offering an assistant professorship in history at Harvard College—an offer Adams at once declined. But the "begonia" attack apparently spurred on the family, which chose to think the "Session" article provoking it hardly an important contribution to American politics:

> . . . No sooner had Adams made at Washington what he modestly hoped was a sufficient success, than his whole family set upon him to drag him away. For the first time since 1861 his father interposed; his mother entreated; and his brother Charles argued and urged that he should come to Harvard College.

Adams capitulated, and, with rancor in his heart and with surely no especial inclination toward his subject, began to teach medieval history at Harvard.

ii

No act of Charles W. Eliot in "reforming" Harvard College is superficially in greater need of justification than the appointment of Henry Adams to teach medieval history. Adams had never written a word upon it nor upon an allied subject. He had shown no aptitude as a scholar, standing well down in his Harvard class and abandoning the study of law in Germany because he could not learn the language. His few articles were on scattered subjects—not to one of them could the epithet "learned" be applied. And at thirty-two he had twice been nationally advertised as frivolous and a lightweight. Why, then, did Dr. Eliot, an astute and farseeing administrator, appoint him?

Not over eager for the appointment, Adams himself challenged the President of Harvard on his selection. "But, Mr. President," urged Adams, "I know nothing about Mediæval History." With the courteous manner and bland smile so familiar to the next generation of Americans, Mr. Eliot mildly but firmly replied, "If you will point out to me any one who knows more, Mr. Adams, I will appoint him." The exact measure of Henry Adams's knowledge of his subject is indicated by the fact that he could think of no American to fill the place which he himself did not want.

The bland smile of Doctor Eliot concealed, of course, an administrative economy and strategy. Ephraim Whitney Gurney, his overworked professor of ancient history and the university's first dean, was making, in the fall of 1870, what might be called a successful marriage, to wealthy Ellen Hooper of Boston, and felt no longer any necessity to conduct the *North American Review* for the stipend it brought. Furthermore, he and Professor Torrey could no longer compass unassisted the range of history demanded by the influx of students and the new styles in curricula. Eliot saw an opportunity to "sandwich-in" a tyro between the energetic Gurney (who was one of the leading reformers at Harvard) and the capable Torrey; and he also saw a chance to make the *North American Review* carry a part of the financial burden of the experiment. Whoever was chosen must be selected with both the review and the college in mind; that person, furthermore, must be acceptable to Gurney. That Dr. Eliot was ruled by the latter is an obvious inference. Justification of the appointment, then, depends upon an analysis of Gurney's motives. How far was he influenced by a desire to strengthen his department at Harvard and improve the review, and how far was he persuaded by gentle pressure from the Adams family?

Debatable as are some of the issues raised by Henry Adams's appointment, the notion that he was established as editor of the *North American Review* for the improvement of that journal is utter nonsense. He had no editorial experience, and Gurney must have foreseen that either he or Lowell (a former editor) would have to oversee Adams's work as an editor. As a matter of fact, the *North American Review* was changed in no important particular while Henry Adams had nominal control of it. Vital changes were made in it as soon as he resigned. The only factor influencing Henry Adams's selection as editor of the review was that he would not be likely to interrupt the important contributions on the railroads begun by his brother in 1867. So far as the *North American Review* was concerned, then, the promotion of the ambitions of Charles Francis Adams, Jr., is the clearest assignable cause for the installation of Henry Adams.

Did Ephraim Gurney consider Henry Adams to be potentially a first-rate medieval historian? One ought not to shout at the idea, for such skepticism makes of the president of Harvard either an idiot or a hypocrite. Where could Eliot have got his opinion that Adams knew as much about the subject of medieval history as any one, except from Gurney? And was Gurney completely deceived? Adams has a revelatory statement in regard to himself in *The Education* that seems to need enlargement: "He knew no history; *he knew only a few historians. . . .*" Henry Adams could claim acquaintance with Stopford Brooke, chaplain-in-ordinary to Queen Victoria and later author of *English Literature from the Beginnings to the Norman Conquest* (1898), and intimacy with "Frank" Palgrave, the eldest son of Sir Francis Palgrave, deputy-keeper of the public records and author of the *History of England: Anglo Saxon Period* (1831) and the *History of Normandy and England,* 4 vols. (1851–1864). "Frank"— Francis Turner Palgrave—was married to the sister of Adams's friend, Charles Milnes Gaskell, and Adams was sufficiently intimate with the Palgrave-Gaskell circle, probably, to talk glibly about the concerns of English medieval historians, in particular about the controversy between the supporters of Sir Francis and those of Edward A. Freeman over the effect of the Norman Conquest on English institutions. We must allow for the possibility that his chatter impressed the less fortunate Ephraim Gurney and that this was the basis of his recommendation to Dr. Eliot. Despite the presence of Norton and Lowell, Harvard College was pleasantly rustic and provincial in 1870.

On the other hand, it will not do to ignore the powerful influence of the Adams family on both Eliot and Gurney. Charles Francis Adams was the most distinguished son of Harvard College in politics in 1870, and Henry's older brother was to become one of the overseers of the institution at the end of the decade. "There is a tradition in the (Hooper) family," writes Ward Thoron, who married into it, "that Gurney, after successfully tutoring Brooks Adams, Henry's younger brother, was recommended by Minister Adams to Dr. Hooper as an excellent person to teach his eldest daughter, who wished to study Greek." If there is any truth in this story of how Gurney met Ellen Hooper (to the improvement of his fortunes), then his gratitude to the father of Henry Adams must be counted a factor in the appointment. If there was no "influence" exerted in Henry's behalf, we have to grant that he displayed a capacity for "politics" on assuming his post that there is no warrant for in his previous career. At the close of his first academic year he wrote Gaskell, "As I have managed to get into the 'inside ring,' as Americans say, the small set of men who control the University, I have things my own way." This was "progress" with a vengeance. Is it not easier to assume that Adams was favored from the start because of his "connections"?

Though the author of *The Education* points out that "it could not much effect the sum of solar energies whether one went on dancing with girls in Washington, or began talking to boys at Cambridge," the *Letters* indicate that Adams felt definitely that his sun was obscured by the clouds in the college town. To Gaskell, he immediately confessed, "I lose by the change. The winter climate is damnable. The country is to my mind hideous. And the society is three miles away in Boston. . . ." He had definitely been "rusticated." Significantly, he celebrated his first holiday—the Christmas recess—by rushing off to Washington. Yet for want of social exercise he went to work. His epistles groan with his labors as he sought to keep ahead of his students in his courses. "My reputation for deep historical research is awful," he whimsically remarked, and we should understand the whimsey of it. He needs must be superficial, but his protection was that his students did not detect how superficial he was:

> . . . As yet I have seen no society. I am too busy and have to read every evening as my young men are disgustingly clever at upsetting me with questions. Luckily I have a little general knowledge which comes in. I gave them the other day a poetical account of Wenlock in relation to Gregory VII and Cluny. You see how everything can be made to answer a purpose.

Wenlock, it must be explained, was a Shropshire abbey converted into a residence (where Adams had frequently stayed) by the Gaskells. The young instructor had knocked about enough to know how to extemporize successfully when necessary. Furthermore, he possessed a ready wit which proved a cheval-de-frise in an emergency. "How were the Popes elected in the eleventh century?" asked Ephraim Emerton in Professor Adams's course. "Pretty much as it pleased God!" was the reply in the instructor's "characteristic and somewhat nasal drawl." The best thing that can be said for Henry Adams is that he did not deceive himself as to his limitations:

> . . . You can imagine me giving lectures on mediæval architecture, cribbed bodily out of Ferguson and Viollet le Duc. Precious lucky it is that Palgrave isn't here to snub me for my intolerable impudence. If he could hear me massacre the principles of historical art, he would . . . brain me where I sit.

So passed the first year of his "professing." He began the second "feeling much more at home in my Mediæval chair than I did a year ago." He still complained of work, but he felt freer to have his fling in society. He found it a "trifle monotonous . . . one is too well known in such a place as this. I am sure every idiocy I ever committed as a boy, is better remembered here than I remember it myself." Adams tried to improve the society of Cambridge himself by innovating new fashions:

> . . . Only last Saturday I made a sensation by giving a luncheon in my rooms here, at which I had the principal beauty of the season and three other buds, with my sister to preside; a party of eleven, and awfully fashionable and larky. They came out in the middle of a fearful snowstorm, and I administered a mellifluous mixture known as champagne cocktails to the young women before sitting down to lunch. . . . They made an uproarious noise and have destroyed forever my character for dignity in the College.

Continuing, Adams intimated to Gaskell that American society could never have the dash of European:

> . . . In this Arcadian society sexual passions seem to be abolished. Whether it is so or not, I can't say, but I suspect both men and women are cold, and love only with great

refinement. How they ever reconcile themselves to the brutalities of marriage, I don't know.

Adams's next letter to Gaskell, on March 26, 1872, told of his engagement to Marian Hooper, sister to Ephraim Gurney's wife and her father's favorite daughter.

In the same year Henry Adams ran his first tilt against a full-fledged medieval historian. "Glance at my notice of Freeman's *Historical Essays* in my next number, if you see it," he begged Gaskell. "I think I have caught him out very cleverly, but I would like to know what you say." Edward Augustus Freeman's *Historical Essays* (1871) is a very important book if one has the object of revealing the whole political background of the scholarly crusade which sought to show the determining influence of German institutions upon the Anglo-Saxon. Incorporating articles written during the Franco-Prussian War, the *Historical Essays* openly takes the side of Germany and castigates Napoleon III for his imperialistic designs. We at once perceive that more than mere scholarship separates the classical school of English historians—Lingard, Hallam, Macaulay, Palgrave, *et al.*—and the Germanist school of Kemble, Freeman, Stubbs, and Green. On one side are arrayed the lovers of ancient and medieval Rome, whose influence they believe spread over Europe and reached England through the invasion of affected races: the particular thesis of Palgrave (the historian most vital to us) being that even the Britons were Continental migrants infected with the ideas of Roman imperialism rather than innocent Celts. Instinctively this school is allied to France, and some of its members to the Roman Church. On the other side, the contention is that all of the free institutions of England are prefigured in German tribal customs, that the Norman Conquest had no effect upon these institutions, and that the normal allegiance of England should be with Germany. Freeman's *Historical Essays* is primarily an anti-French, pro-German tract, with historical studies in Anglo-Germanic history and contemporary political essays significantly intermixed. It is a hand with all the pips exposed.

Adams should have treated the book lightly, perhaps using it to discredit in America the Germanists as a school. Instead he belabored it like Orlando Ponderoso. His partisanship, we feel, is determined wholly by his friendship with the Palgraves and Gaskells. After a conventional and meaningless compliment to Freeman, Adams remarks that the contents of his book "are rather necessary to an elementary education than to the attainment of any very advanced knowledge." "More than half the volume concerns points of continental history," the reviewer continues, "and Mr. Freeman's special grievance . . . is that French ideas of continental history are utterly distorted, and that Englishmen, and we may add Americans, are profoundly ignorant of anything except French ideas. This is not a very lofty aim for an historian of Mr. Freeman's rank. . . ." Adams complains that Freeman assaults the French Empire "with a very vicious temper." He calls Freeman's assertion that Louis Napoleon had used the verbs *révendiquer* and *réunir* in claiming territory which he wished to add to his empire a "wilful, malicious, and unjustifiable calumny of Louis Napoleon Buonaparte, a calumny which must add a considerable sting to the sufferings of that unfortunate man." The critical notice closes with a blast against the competence of Freeman as an historian, a thing hardly warranted by the book under review:

> Barring Mr. Freeman's most inveterate prejudices, he is, when there is neither a French Emperor to abuse nor an Anglo-Saxon king or earl to worship, a hard student and an honest workman. That he is or ever can be a great historian, in any high sense of the word, is difficult to believe. He has read the great German historians, and he probably admires them, but he has certainly failed to understand either their method or their aims. He shows only a limited capacity for critical combinations, and he has a true English contempt for novel theories. In spite of his labors, the history of the Norman Conquest and an accurate statement of Anglo-Saxon institutions still remain as far from realization as ever. . . .

Could it be allowed that Adams is right in some particulars, his review nevertheless is insulting and scurrilous. Perhaps his friends made him feel it was at least undignified. At any rate, the publication of a revised American edition of Freeman's *The History of the Norman Conquest* in 1873 gave him an opportunity to appear better mannered and more erudite. He was well enough pleased with the critical notice which he produced to initial it "H. A." contrary to the practice of his journal. "I have been writing for the next number another little notice of Freeman, calculated to improve his temper as I guess . . . ," he confided to Gaskell. It was a poor guess, if not meant ironically. How did he suppose Freeman would take a review which began with the observation that his major work was "far from attaining its aim so completely" as his *Early English History for Children?*

With raised eyebrows Adams claims "the right to confess a slight feeling of amused disappointment on examining this new and revised edition. The amusement is due to the fact that Mr. Freeman should have discovered in his revision so little to revise; the disappointment to the fact that he should have found nothing to improve." Adams objects to Freeman's overenthusiastic statement that "Aelfred . . . is the most perfect character in history" and to Freeman's attempt to exonerate Earl Godwine from responsibility in the death of another Aelfred, son of Aethelred II. He contends that both the Anglo-Saxon Chronicle and Florence of Worcester establish Godwine's guilt, and that Godwine's "compurgation" later was not equivalent to "acquittal" in any modern sense. The critical notice closes with another prophecy, very similar to that of the first review, dismissing Freeman as an historian:

> . . . If Mr. Freeman proposes to go through all mediæval history in this genial manner, acquitting every man from offence who has ever availed himself of the privilege of compurgation, he will end by offering to the public one of the most considerable lists of hardly treated ruffians and perjurers that has been seen even in this generation, to

which the sight of rehabilitated criminals is so common. But the public patience will hardly last to the end of the list. Its judgment will be that the historian who resorts to such arguments has by the very act abdicated his high office and is no longer entitled to the name. He has become an advocate, and not a very strong one.

Adams has, of course, taken a relatively small incident in *The History of the Norman Conquest* and given it major significance. No one today would presume to say whether Godwine knew that Harold, to whom he surrendered Aelfred, intended to kill the prince, so terse and contradictory are the records. Yet one thing is clear, Freeman had searched the probabilities more thoroughly than had Henry Adams. In the Preface to the third English edition of his work, after an extended rejoinder to Mr. Pearson, Freeman briefly notices his American assailant:

> If I were to examine any anonymous criticism, it would be an article signed "H. A." in the *North American Review*, in which I am blamed for maintaining the innocence of Godwine, though his guilt is asserted in "the Saxon chronicle." It would almost seem as if "H. A." had written this without either looking at the Chronicles themselves or at the examination of their witness in my appendix. Indeed it would seem that, even in such respectable quarters as the *North American Review*, the idea still lingers that there is a single book called "The Saxon chronicle." I need hardly say that strange havoc would be made of history, as strange havoc often has been made, by any one who did not stop to compare the wide difference in statement and feeling between Abingdon and Peterborough.

That Henry Adams was innocent of the fact that there was more than one version of the Anglo-Saxon Chronicle is not the improbability which it seems. In January 1873, he wrote to Henry Cabot Lodge, from Cairo, whither he had gone on his wedding journey, "I have got to learn to read Anglo-Saxon, but that is too much to expect from you or anyone not obliged to do it." Six months later he had just begun the study of the language, which he found "quite amusing." In the same letter, however, he expressed the hope that Lodge would have "more facility" with "Latin and Saxon" than he had—though he saw no necessity for "working very laboriously even at this." Making due allowance for the fact that he was bent on seducing a younger man to pursue a given course of study, one cannot believe that Adams was armed against the egregious blunder he triumphantly produced at the end of the year—for how else may his review be styled?

A three-year interval separated Adams's critical notice and Freeman's Preface, during which time the editor of the *North American Review* and his assistant, Henry Cabot Lodge, scolded the Germanists without effect (as they supposed) in their journal. "I have myself devoted ten pages in my July number to a notice of Prof. Stubbs's unconscionably dull *Constitutional History*," Adams wrote Gaskell in 1874. "And I have ventured to assert some opinions there which I fear that dignified Professor will frown upon. Luckily for me, a good, heavy-bottomed English University Don rarely condescends to notice criticism, and never American criticism. Even Mr. Freeman now ignores my poor comments." There is an unattributable notice of Sir Henry Sumner Maine's *Lectures on the Early History of Institutions* in the *Review* for April 1875, and "H. C. L."—obviously Lodge (who had sole charge of that issue)—has a notice of Kenelm Edward Digby's *An Introduction to the History of Real Property* in the October 1875 number.

These reviews are important as they contain ideas later developed in full in *Essays in Anglo-Saxon Law*, the last carronade that Adams or his students were to discharge at the Freemanites. "The great German historian, Sohm, has described more clearly than Professor Stubbs has done the peculiarities of the Anglo-Saxon political system," declares Adams in his notice of *The Constitutional History of England*. This is a matter of opinion, but it may be significant that no later student has sided with Henry Adams. "So far as private law is concerned," Adams remarks with a glance ahead, "the early history of this great system is almost a blank. Neither Mr. Stubbs nor any other writer has seriously attempted it, and it is destined to remain untouched until Germany has forced England into scholarship." Adams takes the ground that manorial jurisdiction in England was always a mere continuation of hundred jurisdiction. He denies by implication that the English constitution is descended from German tribal law—the Normans surely destroyed the Witan:

> Neither Mr. Stubbs nor even Mr. Freeman would probably maintain that there is any evidence whatever to establish the existence of a legislative assembly under Rufus, Henry I, Stephen, Henry II, Richard, or John. The utmost that can be demonstrated is the occasional indication of a consultive body, which, to say the least, has no stronger affiliations with the Witan than it has with the Curia Regis or the Norman Court of Barons. Two whole centuries elapse between the last meeting of the Witan and the first meeting of Parliament.

The review of Sir Henry Maine's *Lectures* is marked by the reviewer's insistence that primogeniture was a part of the feudal, as distinct from the Germanic, heritage. He poses this query:

> . . . Can Sir Henry demonstrate that at any period whatever the Teutons of the village communities were not absolute owners of the houses in which they lived and the close about those houses? And if English ownership is descended from the ownership of the tribal chief, why were the grants of land in such absolute ownership always acts of the political government, of the king and the people in a legislative capacity?

Lodge, in examining Kenelm Digby's *An Introduction to the History of Real Property*, remarks that "Folcland, the usual stumbling block, has proved one to Mr. Digby" who adopted the view of Kemble and Stubbs that such land was the common property of the nation out of which the king could carve dependent tenures. Lodge holds that, as regards the law, "William the Conqueror superimposed a fully developed system on a half-developed one of the same stock"—the Palgravian thesis.

In these three reviews, whatever their merits and defects, there is the stirring of a small breeze that might have grown to a wind to dissipate the "delusion" which Charles A. Beard has called "one of the weirdest . . . that has ever afflicted American intellectual life, namely, the Teutonic theory of history—the theory that the Teutonic race has been the prime source of political liberty and popular government and that the roots of Anglo-Saxon democracy are to be traced back to tun-moots of barbarians in the forest of northern Germany." Why did not Henry Adams develop his objections to the Freemanites into a general assault upon their master conception? Why was he content to lop off a few of the lower limbs when he might have destroyed it root and branch?

Adams has been extravagantly praised as an historian. "He gave the first historical seminary in this country," asserts Professor Morison. "He was the greatest teacher that I ever encountered," wrote Edward Channing— epitaph enough for any man. The roll of his distinguished students adds lustre to his name—Lodge, Ernest Young, J. Laurence Laughlin, S. M. Macvane, Freeman Snow, Lindsay Swift, Henry Osborn Taylor, Ephraim Emerton, Edward Channing, and Albert Bushnell Hart. Yet Adams undoubtedly missed his greatest opportunity as an historian and teacher. He had neither the strength nor the vision to oppose the Germanists fundamentally.

The contentions of Adams and Lodge in their handling of Freeman, Stubbs, Maine, and Digby in the *North American Review* were in a sense bold guesses. They needed to be substantiated by hard work. "I took the ground in my notice of Stubbs that manorial jurisdiction was *always* a mere continuation of hundred jurisdiction," Adams wrote Lodge in September 1874:

In France the *haute justice* embraced felonies and the *inquisitio*. The constitutional character of English and French feudalism is nicely expressed in this contrast. So we must collect *all* evidence, especially in the reign of Henry II,

who as succeeding the lawless reign of Stephen must have
found manorial power stronger than ever it was again unless
under Henry III. I think I see the way to a good monograph
by you on this point.

This letter, beyond illustrating the element of conjecture
in the critical notices, indicates the beginning of doctoral
studies in history at Harvard. Adams's next missive reports,
"Laughlin of '73 proposes to join our Ph.D. class." It was
the principal work of this class to substantiate the reviews.
Adams told Lodge to indicate to the university authorities
that the course was a "special study on the early English
law as exhibited in Anglo-Saxon and Norman sources, with
a view to ascertaining and fixing the share that Germanic
law had in forming the Common Law." This description
might imply a broader purpose than was ever realized by
Adams and his students.

Employing German methodology, they produced in the
next two years four studies in Anglo-Saxon law, three of
which were offered as doctoral dissertations. Their teacher,
who bore the expense of publication, supplied an initial
study, and in 1876 the lot was printed under the title
Essays in Anglo-Saxon Law. "This has been a really
satisfactory piece of work," Adams wrote Gaskell. "I shall
be curious to learn whether your universities think they
can do better." Certainly there was nothing to compare
with the book as a graduate study either in England or
America at the time. As a permanent contribution to the
history of English law, the book is called valuable by
Winfield. Though there are *lacunae* in the authors'
knowledge, there is no reason to dissent from this estimate.
Our concern is that the book has no broad purpose. It is
not the cornerstone of a structure to be erected athwart the
path of the Germanists. Indeed, Adams can write, "There
is no higher authority on the subject of Anglo-Saxon law
than Dr. Reinhold Schmid. . . ." The book is instead a
specific attack upon the Freemanites as an historical sect,
without any reference to the larger issue, as citation from
Adams's conclusion makes evident (he has just shown that
the Norman-trained Edward the Confessor distributed

powers, especially to the Church, *by writ*, with no reference to the Witan):

> With the hopeless confusion of jurisdictions which followed the collapse caused by the Confessor in the Anglo-Saxon system, this is not the place to deal. From the moment that the private courts of law become a recognized part of the English judicature, the Anglo-Saxon constitution falls to pieces, and feudalism takes its place. Yet whatever historical interest the manorial system possesses, as part of the English judicial constitution, is due to the fact that its origin was not feudal, but Anglo-Saxon. The manor was a private hundred so far as its judicial powers were concerned. The law administered in the manorial courts was hundred law; the procedure was hundred procedure; the jurisdiction, like that of the hundred, was controlled by the shire. The manor was but a proprietory hundred, and, as such has served for many centuries to perpetuate the memory of the most archaic and least fertile elements of both the Saxon and the feudal systems.

That is, the effort of Adams and his students is an effort so to individualize and particularize Anglo-Saxon institutions by insisting on their archaic inflexibility that all liberal elements must be recognized as post-Norman. This could have been made momentous with no more than a turn of phrase, but that phrase was never written or uttered.

Adams, therefore, emerges from his Harvard studies as a mere controversialist. Yet this was precisely how he entered upon them—a partisan of the Palgraves. His quarrel with Freeman began because the publication of the latter's study of the Norman Conquest knocked Palgrave's earlier book off the stocks. Its superior merits Adams never admitted. Later, when the Freemans visited this country and the Adamses met them unexpectedly at the Bancrofts, the Americans appeared to have vied with the guests in being offensive, even in Mrs. Adams's jaundiced account:

> At dinner, the great historian of the Norman Conquest was on my right; Henry *one* removed from my left. Ye Gods, what a feast it was! No stylographic could relate it. Let us

draw a veil over nine-tenths of it. When Freeman informed us that the Falls of Slap-Dash—or some such name—were better worth our seeing than Niagara "for the reason that many streams like your States end in one great *fall*," we let the vile insinuation pass, and Edmunds, with his best senatorial courtesy, said very gently and with no passion in his tones, "Where is this fall, Mrs. Freeman?" "On the Hadriatic," she said, as most Englishwomen would. There was a deathly stillness, unbroken save for the winter rain beating drearily against the window-panes. On we went. The canvasbacks entered. *Three* of them—fresh and fair, done to a turn; and weltering in their gore. Says Mrs. Bancroft, with a growing hauteur of manner as of a turning worm, "Do you appreciate our canvasbacks, Mr. Freeman?" "I cannot eat raw meat," he said angrily, while a convulsive shudder shook his frame. Then the *picador*, which is latent in me when nature is outraged, rose in me, and I said to him, all unconscious of his theories and the scheme of his writing, "I wonder that you do not like rare meat. Your *ancestors*, the Picts and Scots, ate their meat raw and tore it with their fingers." At which he roared out, "O-o-o-o! W*hur* did yer git that?" Unheeding, careless of consequences, I said, "Well, your Anglo-Saxon ancestors if you prefer." He thereupon pawed the air and frothed at the mouth.

The funniest remains to be told, but it must be done viva-voce. It was a dialogue between him and George Bancroft, when the latter was tired and sleepy and at the end of his forces, as the Gauls say. Never having read one line of Freeman, I did not know until the next day the exquisite point of my historical allusions. As I casually repeated them Henry became purple in the face and rolled off his chair, and he, the husband of my bosom, who is wont to yawn affectionately at my yarns, he at intervals of two hours says, "Tell me again what you said to Freeman about the Picts and Scots and Anglo-Saxons." I send this to you for Whitman; to me and to you it is probably without point or flavour. As *we* rose up to go Mrs. Freeman came up to me very kindly and said, "We mean to go *back* to Cambridge before we sail for home to see our friends once more." I smiled like one in a trance and said, "I'm sure they'll be much flattered." That's all; they are at the Arlington, next door, as it were, have been ten days or more, leave tomorrow, and we have neither of us called.

iii

Two quite different explanations are given in *The Education* why Henry Adams resigned his professorship and quit Cambridge for Washington: first, "he regarded himself as a failure," and, secondly, society in the college town was deadly—"a faculty meeting without business." Other motives are assignable from a study of his career: during his last two years at Harvard he had been permitted to offer a course in American history—a course which heightened his already acute sense of the accomplishment of the Adamses. He may have conceived at this time his purpose of writing an historical work which should display the doughty John Quincy Adams as consistently virtuous, even in his "desertion" of the Federalist Party. For this task and for the study of Gallatin upon which he was engaged, the Washington archives were more rewarding than the libraries of Cambridge and Boston. It is likely, too, that if a realization of his limitations as a medieval historian never came to him, some real knowledge of the arduousness of the labors in that field had been borne in upon him. Yet the motive with which he wanted most to impress Gaskell was that of founding a salon in Washington, as Rogers and Milnes had done in the London of an earlier time, and thus "tone-up" society as they had done:

> . . . The fact is I gravitate to a capital by a primary law of nature. This is the only place in America where society amuses me, or where life offers variety. Here, too, I fancy that we are of use in the world, for we distinctly occupy niches which ought to be filled. . . . One of these days this will be a very great city if nothing happens to it. . . . It will be saying in its turn the last word of civilisation. I enjoy the expectation of the coming day, and try to imagine that I am myself, with my fellow *gelehrte* here, the first faint rays of that great light which is to dazzle and set the world on fire hereafter.

Henry Adams's vision of a Washington salon threw a burden upon his wife which life in Cambridge had not imposed. For the first time she assumes an eminence in the narrative not warranted before. Marian Hooper Adams, whom Adams had married in June 1872, was the daughter of the well-to-do Doctor William Hooper and Ellen Sturgis Hooper, an heir to the Sturgis shipping fortune. Katherine Simonds, who in her article, "The Tragedy of Mrs. Henry Adams," has done more towards illuminating our subject than any other critic, makes it clear that this vivacious young woman was a person of great charm and exceptional taste. Her elder sister was described by Henry James as the "exquisite Mrs. Gurney of the infallible taste, the beautiful hands, and the tragic fate"; her brother, Edward William Hooper, treasurer of Harvard College for twenty-two years, was, like Henry Adams, a collector of Chinese paintings. Henry, it seemed, could hardly have done better for a wife; indeed, an acquaintance described theirs as "a marriage of similarities." Nor could so exacting a person as he have had a more satisfactory mistress for his salon.

"Mrs. Adams was an admirable ally to him in making their house a unique place in Washington," writes the celebrated biographer of John Hay. "Sooner or later, everybody who possessed real quality crossed the threshold of 1607 H. Street." Among the élite thus distinguished was an inner circle of friends still more exalted—a clique which included John Hay, William Evarts, and Clarence King. This group became the critics of the Gilded Age, Adams contributing anonymously the novel, *Democracy*, in 1880, and Hay, *The Breadwinners*, in 1883. Adams's novel, whatever its political consequence (and on that he seemed chiefly intent), has little merit as literature, and another novel, called *Esther*, published under the pseudonym "Frances Snow Compton" in 1884, consoles the reader to the fact that Adams wrote no more fiction.

Yet this novel *Esther*, if we follow Miss Simonds, determined Adams's future, for Esther is a portrait of his wife. The novel itself is dull and trivial—the story of a woman who loves a popular minister, but, being a skeptic, cannot marry his church or submit to his faith. It is the severity of the portrait that stuns. Esther, or Marian

Adams, is revealed as a creature of a "gaiety almost too light," a person who, according to Adams, "picks up all she knows without effort, and knows nothing well, yet she seems to understand whatever is said." Though she has "a style of her own," the author can never make up his mind whether he likes it or not. She appears to him to have too little conviction about anything to survive the ordinary tests the spirit is put to:

> . . . I want to know what she can make of life. She gives one the idea of a lightly sparred yacht in mid-ocean unexpected; you ask yourself what the devil she is doing there. She sails gaily along though there is no land in sight and plenty of rough weather coming.

One cannot say, however, that the portrait has no loving touches; on the contrary, Esther appears the product of an exacting love, the love that demands perfection in the object adored. Yet, if the person so portrayed did not comprehend the complex nature of the animus, *Esther* must have fallen as a heavy blow, and there is reason for supposing that Mrs. Adams was in a peculiar psychological condition at the time the book appeared. The devotion of the Adamses to each other is beyond all challenge, yet they were not happy. They had been married twelve years and were still childless. A woman acquaintance says, "Not having any was a greater grief to Mr. Adams than to her," yet this is not certain, for a great change had come to Marian Adams. As a young girl, we are told that, "she did many kind and generous actions," yet later, "she had a reputation for saying bitter things and of unsparingly using her powers of sarcasm whenever an opportunity presented. She was feared rather than loved." Furthermore, Mrs. Adams within a few months after the publication of the book was to lose her father, to whom she was greatly devoted. In Adams's novel Esther likewise loses her parent, a man who, after his retirement, "amused the rest of his life by spoiling this girl." Esther's father, dying, tries in vain to bolster his daughter's courage and strengthen her faith:

"It is not so bad, Esther, when you come to it." But now that she had come to it, it was very bad; worse than anything she had ever imagined; she wanted to escape, to run away, to get out of life itself rather than suffer such pain, such terror, such misery of helplessness.

Who can doubt that here was the suggestion for suicide, and that Mrs. Adams's death on December 6, 1885, from self-administered cyanide must have appeared to the author of the book as the one inevitable result of the portrait? Yet she took her life at a time which she ordinarily gave to writing letters to her father, and it was of him that she was probably thinking rather than of her husband, the author of *Esther*. Adams had no assurance of this, however, nor could he be certain that his disappointment in regard to children was not a factor in his wife's rash act. Perhaps, too, the recollection of his persistent banter on the subject of sexual freedom, with its unmeant implication of lack of satisfaction in his wife, may have oppressed Adams as a factor in her death:

> Such a quaint little society, you never saw or imagined. We do not even talk scandal. There is no scandal to talk about. . . . We are all of the Darby and Joan type, and attached to our wives. It is the fashion. . . .

Yet if he ever chid himself for frivolity in talk on this subject, his intimates had no knowledge of it. When, in time, he was to reëstablish himself as a gracious host in Washington, John Hay could chaff him, without any idea of offense, on the score of his success with the ladies. "*Ces dames* are desolate without you." It is only when we see beneath the polished surface of *Mont-Saint-Michel and Chartres*, privately printed in 1904, and after wide circulation and discussion given to the general public in 1913, that we understand how hard Adams was hit.

To appreciate fully Adams's second excursion into medievalism we must pick up and follow a very faint trail. It begins in Paris in January 1891, when we find Adams trying to absorb the French Naturalists. "Imagine my state of happiness," he writes to Elizabeth Cameron, "surrounded by a pile of yellow literature, skimming a volume of Goncourt, swallowing a volume of Maupassant with my roast, and wondering that I feel unwell afterwards." By his process of reading at least a volume a day, Adams came to Joris-Karl Huysmans, an author who may have repelled him, but in whom he maintained an interest for twenty years.

Huysmans's career was to have certain parallels with Adams's own, parallels he could appreciate better than any one else, and Huysmans had treated, and was to treat, certain subjects of especial interest to Adams. Huysmans began his career as a Naturalist, a believer in Positivism, and a follower of Goncourt and Zola. He had, at the outset, as firm a conviction in the value of science as Adams. Then came the sophisticated and audacious satire of the Decadents in *A Rebours*, a volume which plausibly may have appealed to Adams because of its cynical tone and its profession of admiration for what was decadent.

At the time when Adams was reading yellow-backed novels in Paris, however, the Huysmans book which was most likely to fall into his hands was *La Bas*, over which Paris was still agitated, though the volume had appeared the year before *Esther* was published. *La Bas* is a disgusting book, an effort to pile refuse on the High Altar, and, while its skepticism may have appealed to Adams's mood, it could not have been this which permanently attracted Adams to the book. There is, first of all, in *La Bas* a hatred of the nineteenth century; even occultism, Huysmans insists, has degenerated since the Middle Ages. "The people," one character says, "grow from century to century more avaricious, abject, and stupid." And again, "Society has done nothing but deteriorate in the four centuries separating us from the Middle Ages." *La Bas* denounces the "Americanisms" that Henry Adams detested in the America of Grant's administration. The Catholic general, Boulanger, so much like Grant, is denounced for "American" methods of self-advertisement; Huysmans even insists that Gilles de Rais's death at the stake is to be preferred to an "American lynch-law" death.

Very important in the book is Huysmans's attack upon Joan of Arc. If Joan had only stayed with her mother, France would not have become a heterogeneous nation; the Charles she saved was the leader of Mediterranean cutthroats, not Frenchmen at all, but Latins—Spaniards and Italians. Without Joan, Northern France and England would have remained united, a homogeneous nation of Normans. Now this is a most important passage for the development of Henry Adams's thinking. When we are invited to visit Mont-Saint-Michel by the author, it is on the score that, if we have any English blood at all, we are also Norman, with an hypothetical ancestry of two hundred and fifty million in the eleventh century, ploughing the fields of Normandy, rendering military service to the temporal and spiritual lords of the region, and helping to build the Abbey Church. Adams was inordinately proud of his Norman ancestry, and in that highly personal poem, *Prayer to the Virgin of Chartres*, which was found among his papers after his death, he even fancies himself "an English scholar with a Norman name" returning to France in the thirteenth century to study in the schools and worship at the shrine of the Virgin.

Finally, Adams found in *La Bas*—though he may not have been immediately attentive to it—a skepticism in regard to science more deeply felt than Huysmans's hostility toward the Church. In the nineteenth century, says Huysmans, speaking through the character Gevingey, "People believe nothing, yet gobble everything." Positivism, the first love of Huysmans, is roundly denounced. Barbey d'Aurevilly had prophesied after reading À *Rebours* that Huysmans would choose either "the muzzle of a pistol or the foot of the cross," and to the discerning this choice was possibly even more apparent in *La Bas*. To Henry Adams, however, it must have come as something of a surprise to find that the irreverent writer who had fascinated him in *La Bas* had set off in 1892 to be converted at a Trappist monastery. He read the story in Huysmans's novel *En Route* (1895); and followed it through the highly symbolical novel, *La Cathedral* (1898), from which he several times quotes in *Mont-Saint-Michel and Chartres*; reaching finally *L'Oblat* in 1903. *Les Foules de Lourdes* (1906), with its discussion of the many shrines erected in southern France to the Virgin, which to the casual reader seems most like Adams, came out too late to have exerted any influence upon him. If Adams interpreted the writing of *La Bas* as an act which drove Huysmans back to Catholicism in contrition, he could not but realize another parallel between himself and the Frenchman—both had written a novel of which they deeply repented.

Yet Adams could not readily produce a series of Catholic novels, as Huysmans had done, by way of atonement. His sin was in his eyes, perhaps, not specifically against the Church, but against Woman. Hence, *Mont-Saint-Michel and Chartres* is one of the most eloquent tributes to the power of Woman ever penned by man. For whatever she may have meant to the thirteenth century, and whatever she continues to mean to the devout, the Virgin symbolized for Adams Woman Enthroned. He writes with scarcely less eloquence when he treats of the three great queens of France, Eleanor of Guienne, Mary of Champagne, and Blanche of Castile, at whose courts poetry and courtesy were born. They brought to the political and social world the order and unity Adams so much admired. Whether he writes of the legendary windows or of Nicolette and Marion, it is the feminine influence on glass and "chante-fable" that interests him. In the world that he reveals Woman is everywhere triumphant and supreme. The book, *Mont-Saint-Michel and Chartres,* should not be looked upon, possibly, as a study in medieval history, but rather as a cathedral of words— various, complex, and beautiful, yet designed to give a single impression—a cathedral erected by Henry Adams to the glory of Womankind.

Absurdly futile, then, the scholar's effort to show that Adams used in the main secondary sources for his book. Equally futile also to suggest that Adams discovered a unity and order in France in the era of cathedral building which may not have been so apparent to contemporaries. And even a little ridiculous to charge Adams, as a modern historian, with neglect of economics in his study. The reference ought not to be from *Mont-Saint-Michel and Chartres* to thirteenth-century France, to test Adams's accuracy, but to contemporaneous works of literature, to fix the place and meaning of the book, for Adams's creation is a prose poem rather than anything else. Yet the first and most obvious reference—to James Russell Lowell's *The Cathedral*—is not very rewarding. Here Adams may have found approval for his love of Gothic Chartres, the coupling of philosophy with aesthetic meditation, yet withal a stout protestantism which may have helped him to resist neo-Thomism. There is just a chance, moreover, that he may have transmuted Lowell's "genius," whom the poet represents as feminine, into the ubiquitous American "niece" whose presence is so very incongruous in *Mont-Saint-Michel and Chartres:*

> But she, my Princess, who will some day deign
> My garret to illumine till the walls. . .
> Dilate. . . .
> One feast for her I secretly designed
> In that Old World so strangely beautiful
> To us the disinherited of eld,—
> A day at Chartres, with no soul beside
> To roil with pedant prate my joy serene
> And make the minster shy of confidence.

An utterly absurd idea—yet no more absurd than the presence of the niece herself, hence worth retaining.

The more we reflect upon it, the more it seems imperative to explain Henry Adams's choice of a companion for his last medieval excursion. An American niece! To be sure, Adams had nieces, but one would not thoughtlessly take one's *own* niece into the thirteenth century. She must have been, in Adams's imagination, some unattached Daisy Miller—such as his friend Henry James invented and piloted with eleemosynary regard through Europe. Yet she must have potentialities which the novelist had not observed. Adams could not read James's novels. "James knows almost nothing of women but the mere outside; he never had a wife." James's heroines were crushed or absorbed by their European experiences; Adams wanted a young woman who could survive the text he chose for the day. He had much to accomplish still, and the years had taught him that, though he had the strength of the Archangel, he could accomplish nothing without her. A melancholy letter to Henry James, on November 18, 1903, elicited by the novelist's study of a *"type bourgeois-bostonien,"* tells of Adams's discovery "at least thirty years ago"—the time of the Washington salon—that they were but "improvised Europeans." An American society could not be created by male shams. If his *ingenue,* however, were capable of learning enough from the women of the thirteenth century to go back to her own country to create a society which she through her sex should dominate, then Adams's life would not be as fruitless as it seemed. A sex-conscious Daisy might conquer the earth, and to awaken her it was worth while to parade the pertinent lore of a forgotten century. Was ever medievalism put to so exalted a purpose?

AFTERWORD

The question must fairly occur to some readers, How does a pluralistic criticism differ from a well-documented piece of research? The answer is revealed by contrasting this essay with its predecessor. It is, in the main, monistic in its approach. Written a decade earlier than the Whitman effort, it draws on no earlier criticism or scholarship aside from Katherine Simonds' article, for none existed. Henry Steele Commager was to write well on Adams as an American historian, Max Baym was to explore Adams' French sources (largely secondary), and Ernest Samuels was to produce his three-volume biography—all in the future. My topic was dictated, since whatever I wrote had to be appropriate for a *Festschrift* for one of my former teachers at Stanford, the medievalist

Carleton Brown. Only the concluding portion gets away from the direct method of simple research and evaluation; there, however, I do bring in a comparison between Adams and the Huysmans of *The Cathedral* period that possibly has some force. American critics very gingerly use the comparative method unless it reflects to the credit of their subject. This tendency I combatted in *Intellectual America*, daring to hint that some American products were derivative and inferior. I do not go that far here, for I deeply admire *Mont-Saint-Michel and Chartres*, though I have very mixed feelings about its author. The elaborate self-pity of *The Education* offends me. I felt Adams to be very light-weight as a young man and was so eager to set this forth that I indulged in "over-kill" in two-thirds of the essay, not reserving space enough for proper consideration of Adams' major work—a weakness pointed out to me by Howard Mumford Jones. Yet how could I help being exercised over a man who was a racist, a disciple of Taine (the most persuasive of 19th century racists), and whose letters—the unpublished ones—contain many an anti-semitic charge and inuendo? The essay is much too long; it is criticism, fully as much as poetry, that should be short enough to be read at one sitting.

4   WILLIAM DEAN HOWELLS
AS
HENRY JAMES'S "MORAL POLICEMAN"

i Opening the Door

The longest important association in American letters was that of William Dean Howells and Henry James. In the beginning it was the friendship between a young writer of fiction, eager for a regular outlet, and the newly appointed assistant editor of the magazine which each was most willing should prosper. Howells, as Fields's junior on the *Atlantic Monthly*, had the realization of James's hopes in his hands, and to judge from the letter which James wrote to be read at the party in New York City honoring Howells on his seventy-fifth birthday, on March 2, 1912, James felt he could not have had a more sympathetic friend in power:

> My debt to you began well nigh half a century ago in the most personal way possible, and then kept growing and growing with your own admirable growth—but always rooted in the early intimate benefit. This benefit was that you held out your open editorial hand to me at the time I began to write—and I allude especially to the summer of 1866—with a frankness and sweetness of hospitality that was really the making of me, the making of the confidence that required help and sympathy and that I should other-wise, I think, have strayed and stumbled about a long time without acquiring. You showed me the way and opened me the door; you wrote me and confessed yourself struck with me—I have never forgotten the beautiful thrill of *that*. You published me at once. . . .

This assumption of cordiality is borne out by Howells's earlier reminiscence. James "had already printed a tale— 'The Story of a Year'—in the *Atlantic Monthly*," Howells recalled not quite accurately, "when I was asked to be Mr. Fields's assistant in the management, and it was my fortune to read Mr. James's second contribution in manuscript. 'Would you take it?' asked my chief. 'Yes, and all the stories you can get from the writer.' One is much securer in one's judgment at twenty-nine than, say, at forty-five; but if this was a mistake of mine I am not yet old enough to regret it. The story was called 'Poor Richard.' " But the most substantial proof that Howells "opened me the door" is, of course, the publishing record. As assistant editor of the *Atlantic* (March 1, 1866–1871) and as editor-in-chief (July 1, 1871–Feb. 2, 1881), Howells accepted from Henry James and published five novels, six *novelle*, seven short stories, a farce, eight art articles, eight travel sketches, and six reviews and notices. One of these novels, *The American*, Howells induced Francis P. Church, editor of the *Galaxy*, to turn over to him after learning from James himself that he would have preferred to send it to the *Atlantic*, being dissatisfied with the owners of the *Galaxy*. James had sent the story to the New York magazine because he had felt the timing inopportune for the *Atlantic*. *The Europeans* was in the hands of the *Galaxy* for serial publication at the time of its merger with the *Atlantic* and was also turned over to the surviving magazine. Despite this fortuitous arrival of one of James's serials Howells was, on this showing, the friendliest of James's editors.

Howells's receptivity to James's work was fostered in a period of close communication with the younger man, which began probably in the fall of 1866 when the Jameses returned from Swampscott. "I cannot recall my first meeting with Henry James, or for that matter, the second or third or specifically any after meeting," Howells wrote in 1920. "All I can say is that we seemed presently to be always meeting, at his father's house and at mine, but in the kind Cambridge streets rather than those kind Cambridge houses which it seems to me I frequented more than he. We seem to have been presently always together, and always talking methods of fiction, whether we walked the streets by day or night, or we sat together reading our stuff to each other; his stuff which we both hoped might make itself into matter for the *Atlantic Monthly,* then mostly left to my editing by the senior editor Mr. Fields." In regard to the substance of those frequent and protracted dialogues on "the methods of fiction" Howells gives us only one further hint, which, however, may be of the utmost importance:

> We [Howells and his wife] were of like Latin sympathies, he [James] was inveterately and intensely French, and with the Italian use of our three or four years' life in Italy we could make him feel that we met on a common ground. James could not always keep his French background back, and sometimes he wrote English that the editor easily convicted of Gallicism; but this was the helplessness of early use and habit from his life and school in France throughout boyhood.
> . . . I had learned to like his fiction from such American subjects as *Poor Richard,* but now it was such a French theme as *Gabrielle de Bergerac* which had employed his art. . . . We were sufficiently critical no doubt as an editorial family should be, but we richly felt the alien quality and circumstance of the tales and novels which I eagerly accepted from him. . . .

It would appear from this that some of the discussions between James and his editor may have revolved on the question of how far it was appropriate to write and to print in America any fiction which was "French" in its character. Howells was not the only one at this time to object to the Gallicisms in James's prose; his brother William protested against them and so did J. C. Heywood in the New York *Sun;* but the French "background" which James could not always keep "back" was more than scattered Gallicisms in his style—it was "the alien quality and circumstances" of the tales as well. Fields had apparently warned Howells against the young contribu-

tor's penchant for pessimism and Howells, amused, had
repeated the proprietor's words to James. The latter had
begun his career with a sensational story of a French
mistress who, in plotting the death of her husband,
achieved the death of her lover. *Gabrielle de Bergerac*,
which Howells cites as having disturbed him and his wife,
tells the story of a girl who elopes with her tutor because
the tutor has been wrongly accused by her brother of
making her his mistress and subsequently has been dismissed. Yet it should be noted that Howells published this
novella despite Fields's caution and despite its theme.

That Howells should have had qualms about issuing a
tale of wrongfully accused innocence is not surprising to
those who have been made acquainted with his neurotic
prudery. Yet Howells was very conscious of his limitation
and at times struggled against it. Prior to going to Venice
as consul in the Civil War, Howells had contributed
Heinesque poems and, in defiance of "the Misses Nancy of
criticism," an essay of qualified approval of Whitman to
the *Saturday Press*—that notorious outlet for the New
York bohemians. He may have even hoped that Henry
Clapp and his cohorts might adopt him, for he went to
New York to meet them but was completely discouraged,
according to Professor Cady, by his reception. Italy and
marriage to Elinor Mead, relative of John Humphrey
Noyes and sister to a sculptor, should not have put great
obstacles in the way of his self-improvement. At any rate,
when Howells returned to America and established himself in New York as a free lance, he again made overtures
to the *Saturday Press* through the device of praise for it in
his "Letter from New York" in the Cincinnati *Daily
Gazette*. It was during this tentative period in New York
that Howells made his only lasting enemy by attacking
that syrupy mound of respectability, Dr. Josiah Gilbert
Holland. It was to this incipient, but hesitant, mild
iconoclast, with his common "Latin sympathies," that the
young James appealed—and appealed persuasively enough
to get *Gabrielle de Bergerac* published.

Ironically, Howells was treated to his most drastic lesson

in public taste during this very period of his presentation of his more venturesome young protégé in the pages of his magazine, when at the urgency of Dr. Holmes, but with the disapprobation of James Russell Lowell, he published, while Fields was in Europe, "The True Story of Lady Byron's Life" by Harriet Beecher Stowe in the *Atlantic* in September, 1869. Howells may have been afraid to reject it for fear of losing so important a contributor, he may have yielded too readily to Holmes (another important contributor), but on the whole, his reasons for publishing the story are almost as strange as Mrs. Stowe's in writing it. Perhaps in part it was a boldness inspired by association with a more emancipated, younger man. "Howells seemed to approve," says James C. Austin. "The public reaction to the article was far beyond anything the *Atlantic* had ever gone through." The magazine and the author were abused and subscriptions were canceled wholesale. The effect of this, if not to shock Howells back into prudery, was to teach him an extraordinary editorial caution. No more daring adventures for the *Atlantic* in the field of morals.

On the score of what the public would accept, Henry James would have had every inclination to defer to his editor. "James was younger, his experience of the world of men and the practical world in which one sold and published writing much less than Howells'." That Howells, despite his generous reception of James's work, increasingly annoyed James by persistent criticism of the "immoral" implications of his tales, especially after the Lady Byron episode, and by his pressure on the author to respect the tabus of his age is not beyond demonstration. Howells actually refused only one story from James in fifteen years but that possibly for the wrong reasons. If the story was "The Light Man," with its patently assumed sophistication and cynicism, Howells could have rejected it for its clumsy narrative method—that of longish diary entries—but he probably objected to its tone. A more irritating episode, possibly, occurred in connection with the publication of "The Madonna of the Future." James, who was traveling, evidently entrusted proofreading on this contribution to his father. Howells objected to the length of the tale, and "besides he had a decided shrinking from one episode—that in which Theobald tells his love for, and his visit from the Titian-ic beauty, and his subsequent disgust with her worthlessness, as being risky for the magazine; and . . . he objected to the interview at the end between the writer and the old English neighbor, as rubbing into the reader what was sufficiently evident without it." James's father conceded that Howells was "too timid" in both cases, yet he consented to the deletion of two episodes on the provision that the editor run the remainder in a single issue. Howells revised the tale to cover the deletions and this was the way in which it appeared. James naturally resented this tampering with his work, but he had to assent to it:

> With such a standard of propriety, it makes a bad look-out ahead for imaginative writing. For what class of minds is it that such very timorous scruples are thought necessary? . . . Evidently Howells has a better notion of the allowances of the common public than I have, and I am much obliged to him for performing the excision personally, for of course he will have done it neatly.

Howells added fuel to James's resentment by telling him, after the tale had been published, that, much as he liked the piece, he found "the insistence on the cats and monkeys philosophy" a blemish, and later, when he reviewed the volume in which it was collected, laid precisely the same stricture on the story. James may well have concluded that Howells's caution ran beyond the reticence of his readers. Yet, when Howells objected to the ending of *The American* (which, however, he allowed James to keep), James, while defending the verisimilitude of his conclusion, conceded, "But whether the *Atlantic* ought to print unlimited tragedy is another question— which you are doubtless quite right in regarding as you do. Of course, you couldn't have for the present another evaporated marriage from me! I suspect it is the tragedies in life that arrest my attention more than the other things and say more to my imagination."

But if James conceded to Howells that his editor knew more about public taste than he did, he thought highly neither of that taste nor of its zealous guardian, though he concealed his feelings from the latter. In writing to Grace Norton on November 27, 1870, he allowed his estimate of Howells's timidity to color his evaluation of him as a writer.

> Poor Howells is certainly difficult to defend, if one takes a standpoint the least bit exalted; make any serious demands and its all up with him. He presents, I confess, to my mind, a somewhat melancholy spectacle—in that his charming style and refined intentions are so poorly and meagrely served by our American atmosphere. There is no more inspiration in an American journey than that! Thro' thick and thin I continue however to enjoy him—or rather thro' thin and thinner. There is a little divine spark of fancy which never quite gives out. . . .

To Charles Eliot Norton, an especial friend of Howells then in Europe, James wrote in January, 1871, to praise Howells's *Suburban Sketches* as belonging, "by the wondrous cunning of their manner, to very good literature" and to admit that American civilization might provide, up "to a certain point a very sufficient literary field." He added, however, that "it will yield its secrets only to a really *grasping* imagination. This I think Howells lacks." After Howells became editor-in-chief of the *Atlantic*, James wrote the same correspondent:

> Howells is now monarch absolute of the *Atlantic* to the increase of his profit and comfort. His talent grows constantly in fineness but hardly, I think, in range of application. I remember your saying some time ago that in a couple of years when he had read Sainte-Beuve & c. he would come to his best. But the trouble is he will never read Sainte-Beuve, nor care to. He has little intellectual curiosity, so here he stands with his admirable organ of style, like a poor man holding a diamond and wondering how he can wear it. It's rather sad I think. . . .

The unfairness of this comment reveals that James's annoyance was deep; later in the seventies, as Leon Edel has amusingly shown, James deliberately started teasing Howells indirectly about his narrowness. On February 3, 1876, he told Howells that Edmond de Goncourt contemplated writing a novel on "a whore-house *de province*." To which, Howells responded that he thanked God that he wasn't a Frenchman. In his next letter, on May 28, 1876, James told how he had been visiting in Paris the supposedly illegitimate daughter of an English peer, a certain Baroness:

> She lives in a queer old mouldy, musty *rez-de-chaussée* in the depths of the Faubourg St. Germain, is the greasiest and most audacious lion huntress in all creation, and has two most extraordinary little French emancipated daughters. One of these, wearing a Spanish mantilla and got up apparently to dance the cachacha, presently asked me what I thought of *incest* as a subject for a novel—adding that it had against it that it was getting, in families, so terribly common.

"We do not know," Edel remarks, "whether Howells made any rejoinder on this occasion." Edel misses the deadly thrust in this, however—the reminder to Howells that he had printed the most notorious allegation of incest of the century in the Byron case. Edel does report, on the other hand, how James "with unconcealed delight" had told that "a mother, after reading a novel by Howells, took elaborate precautions that it should not be read by her daughter. It seemed to James a pleasant irony that a novel by a writer scrupulously careful to keep his work 'wholesome,' who pleaded for happy endings and simple romantic tales from him, should be forbidden a *jeune fille*."

Coupled with Howells's efforts to persuade James to be less venturesome in challenging the limitations of magazine fiction was pressure on the younger man to adopt Hawthorne as a model. Miss Kelley, who first noted the existence of this pressure, observes that, although Howells shared with James an interest in George Eliot, Howells confessed that he found a "more potent charm" in

Hawthorne's "more artistic handling" of the problem of evil than he found in George Eliot's treatment. If the issue of Hawthorne's adumbration of evil were ever a contention between the two men—and one cannot help feeling that it was—then James's extended preferential comparison of J. G. Lockhart's *Adam Blair* with *The Scarlet Letter* in his critical study of Hawthorne was intended more for the eye of Howells than for that of any other reader:

> *Adam Blair* is the history of the passion, and *The Scarlet Letter* the history of its sequel. . . . I confess that a large portion of the interest of *Adam Blair*, to my mind . . . , lay in noting its difference of tone. It threw into relief the passionless quality of Hawthorne's novel, its element of cold and ingenious fantasy, its elaborate imaginative delicacy. These things do not constitute a weakness in *The Scarlet Letter*; indeed in a certain way they constitute a great strength; but absence of something warm and straightforward, a trifle more grossly human and vulgarly natural, which one finds in *Adam Blair*, will always make Hawthorne's tale less touching to a large number of even very intelligent readers, than a love-story told with the robust, synthetic pathos which served Lockhart so well.

But one should note also James's insistence that "Lockhart's story is *as decent, as severely draped*, as *The Scarlet Letter*. . . ." The stories and novels of James certainly deal with passion in a warmer, more natural and direct way, while still keeping it decently draped, than do those of Hawthorne. If this were a result of the long discussions with Howells, then Howells contributed to James's development by providing him with a foil before he demonstrated his skill to the public.

One contribution of Howells to the younger man, however, is so patent as to need no demonstration—he improved James's style. The Gallicisms that we have noted gradually disappeared; James's prose became more simple and supple—the result was that in the 1880's these two American novelists were writing the best narrative prose in English.

ii "Finer . . . than . . . Dickens and Thackeray"

Of the practicing critics who treated his work over the years, Henry James owed most, probably, to William Dean Howells. It was Howells who regularly dropped into his writing encomiums for James's fictions, who kept interest in him perpetually alive. James "is . . . extremely gifted — gifted enough to do better than anyone has yet done toward making us a real American novel," Howells wrote Stedman at the end of 1866. "Each one of Mr. Henry James's books is as broad as any one of Balzac's; and we believe his *Princess Casamassima* is of a scope and variety quite unknown to them," he observed in a general essay in 1887. Yet it was Howells who, with the best intentions in the world as critic, created the greatest difficulty for James as an artist dependent on his pen. Moreover, though Howells was generally laudatory, the reservations that he voiced were peculiarly irritating to James and outweighed the praise when relations between the two men were strained. Thus the comment in Howells's review of A *Passionate Pilgrim and Other Tales* that "it would be better if the assumed narrator were able to keep himself from seeming to patronize the simpler-hearted heroes, and from openly rising above them in a worldly way" probably stuck longer in James's memory than Howells's praise of the whole collection: "[these stories] remain to us a marvel of workmanship. In richness of expression and splendor of literary performance, we may compare him with the greatest, and find none greater than he. . . ." Or such a moralistic quibble as that over Monsieur de Mauves's advice to his wife to take a lover: "a difficulty with so French a situation is that only a French writer can carry due conviction of it to the reader. . . ."

Impressed as Howells was with James's fiction, he thought very little of him as a critic, writing of *French Poets and Novelists:*

> His reviews of other writers are not precisely criticism, but they possess a pleasant flavor of criticism, agreeably

diffused through a mass of sympathetic and often keenly analytical impressions. It is saying a great deal when we admit that he reminds us more of Sainte-Beuve than any other English writer; but he is more of a *causeur* than the author of the famous *Causeries,* and less of a critic in a systematic sense.

Though he called James's *Hawthorne* "a delightful and excellent essay, refined and delicate in perception, generous in feeling, and a worthy study of the unique romancer," Howells really emphasized in his feature review the common American reaction and may have been thought to have stimulated it:

> Forty-six, fifty, sixty-four, are not dates so remote, nor are Salem and Concord societies so extinct, that the people of those places cannot [*sic*] be safely described as provincial, not once, but a dozen times; and we foresee, without any very powerful prophetic lens, that Mr. James will be in some quarters promptly attainted of high treason. . . . We think the epithet is sometimes mistaken. . . . If Hawthorne was "exquisitely provincial" one had better take one's chance of universality with him than with almost any Londoner or Parisian of his time. . . . It is not enough to say of a book so wholly unexampled and unrivaled as *The Scarlet Letter* that it was "the finest piece of imaginative writing put forth in America"; as if it had its parallel in any literature. . . .

Close publication of *Daisy Miller* and of Howells's *The Lady of the Aroostook,* with their somewhat similar "international" heroines, Daisy and Lydia Blood, in situations alike challenging to their reputations, led readers, especially British readers, to link the two American authors together. Howells's treatment of the English uncle, Henshaw Erwin, in his novel, and James's *An International Episode* tied them further in the satirical handling of English folk, aroused resentment, and led to their being labeled the "new [American] School" as early as 1880.

At this inopportune time Howells, who suffered a real Anglophobia, was invited to write a long appreciative article on "Henry James Junior" in which he compared the

American author with the best established English novel-ists, all to the advantage of the former.

It seems to me that an enlightened criticism will recognize in Mr. James's fiction a metaphysical genius working to aesthetic results. . . . No other novelist, except George Eliot, has dealt so largely in an analysis of motive, has so fully explained and commented upon the springs of action in the persons of the drama, both before and after the facts. These novelists are more alike than any others in their processes, but with George Eliot an ethical purpose is dominant, and with Mr. James an artistic purpose. . . . Isabel has her great weaknesses, as Dorothea had, but these seem to me, on the whole, the most nobly imagined and the most nobly intentioned women in modern fiction; and I think Isabel is the more subtly divined of the two. . . .

It is a little odd . . . [that James's] power of engaging your preference for certain of his people has been so little commented on. Perhaps it is because he makes no obvious appeal for them. . . . [It] comes about through their own qualities, and is not affected by insinuation or by downright petting, such as we find in Dickens nearly always and in Thackeray too often.

The art of fiction has, in fact, become a finer art in our day than it was with Dickens and Thackeray. We would not suffer the confidential attitude of the latter now, nor the mannerism of the former, any more than we could endure the prolixity of Richardson or the coarseness of Fielding. These great men are of the past—they and their methods and interests; even Trollope and Reade are not of the present. The new school derives from Hawthorne and George Eliot rather than any others. . . . This school . . . finds its chief exemplar in Mr. James. . . .

"I suppose you have seen that I have stirred up the English papers pretty generally by what I wrote of Dickens and Thackeray in my paper on James," Howells wrote Roswell Smith, on November 19, 1882, from Switzerland. "I don't remember what I said, but so far as they have quoted me, I stand by myself, and should only wish to amplify and intensify the opinions that they object to. I knew what I was talking about, and they don't know at all what they are talking about."

Howells had indeed stirred up indignation in England. Leading off with a review of Howells's *A Modern Instance* in 1882, the *Graphic* stigmatized the book as "a typical novel of the newest fashion," written "in the celebrated manner of Henry James, Junior, which consists of saying nothing in a great many words." John Nichol, concluding his *American Literature, An Historical Sketch, 1620–1880*, felt impelled to warn James and Howells jointly against their method: "Together they stand in peril of betraying their mission by overworking their mines." The *Quarterly Review* was caustic. Contrasting the "charm and beauty" of Frances Hodgson Burnett's *Louisiana* with the "artificial mannerisms" and "tawdry smartness" of *Daisy Miller*, it raised the question of whether James was even qualified to report on "American" character types, since, as Howells had indicated in the biographical notes in his article, James was of Irish and Scots descent and did not even live in America. It castigated the lack of story in his "studies" and found only "philosophical instruction and dawdling sentimentality." The *Portrait of a Lady*, for example, was simply "dull, unspeakably dull." As for the slur on Dickens and Thackeray, one could remember their characters, but who could recall one of the *personae* of Howells? Arthur Tilley, in "The New School of Fiction" in the *National Review*, echoed the *Quarterly's* strictures on lack of plot and of vital motive and on labored analysis but was more moderate in tone. The *Spectator* mocked James with an idea and phrase it picked up from James's review of *The Correspondence of Carlyle and Emerson* in the *Century*: "In Mr. Henry James's view of life . . . we have the lowest form of the rapidly dwindling Puritanic faith, a thin sort of pessimism. . . ." Karl Hillebrand in the *Contemporary Review*, citing Howells's opinion of Dickens and Thackeray, lumped Howells and James as "North Americans in whom this ignoring of the past and forgetting of all proportion show themselves most crudely." Simultaneously *Temple Bar* published an essay, "The New School of Fiction," which found these writers possessed of "futility" and "tenuity" and lacking "red blood." James's *Portraits of*

Places, appearing in 1884, was patronizingly reviewed and his *Tales of Three Cities* drew from the *Pall Mall Budget* the opinion that by adding two tales and one city, James had made no improvement on Dickens: his form was "infinitely conceited" and his subjects "infinitely trivial."

James had returned to America, after an absence of six years, late in 1881; he was called to Boston from Washington by the illness of his mother and, following her death, made that city his headquarters until May when he returned to England. On March 18, 1882, Howells wrote John Hay on the cordial renewal of his friendship:

> Henry James is spending the winter only a few doors from us. (We left our country house after my sickness, and came into town.) I see him constantly, and we talk literature perpetually, as we used to do in our walks ten years ago. He is not sensibly changed, and, reflected in him, I find that I am not.

James returned to London in May and in July secured lodgings in South Kensington for the Howellses, who were to have a holiday in England and Europe. In mid-September, Howells, reporting his felicity, attributed it largely to the younger novelist: "H. J., Jr., has been an adoptive father in housing and starting this orphan family in London. Just now he has gone to France." The Howellses themselves left immediately after for Switzerland to spend two months on Lake Geneva, and it would appear that the essay "Henry James Junior" was written at Villeneuve. James could have had no time to examine it or realize its effect on his return to London in December, for he was called back to the United States "almost at once" by a message announcing the serious illness of his father. He could not have fully comprehended the storm Howells had raised in England until his return there in August, 1883. Before this, Howells had written to Thomas S. Perry, from Florence, regretting his paper *so far as it had involved James in controversy,* with the hope, perhaps, that Perry would convey this thought to James. There is no evidence that he did:

The British lion . . . seems to have been born . . . without a cuticle. It is only necessary to insinuate that all English novels are not perfection. One of my London friends actually asked me if I didn't hate Thackeray and Dickens because they were English! . . . I have been scarcely if at all troubled by the row about me, and *have been chiefly vexed because it includes James*.

James showed no immediate inclination to disavow the connection Howells had forced on him. A summary article on "Anthony Trollope" in the *Century Magazine* for July, 1883, connected that novelist, who had just died, with Dickens and Thackeray (though ranking him beneath them) but marked his demise as "the complete extinction of his school." James castigated Trollope for writing too much—his "fertility was gross, importunate," and for an utter lack of a sense of form—"it is probably safe to affirm that he had no 'views' whatever on the subject of novel-writing." Here was much to cause English readers to align him with Howells. A month later, differing with Warner on the primary purpose of the novel, which Warner had maintained to be entertainment, James had insisted that it is to "represent life" and had said that *some* got this illusion from the novels of Miss Austen, others from those of Dumas, and still others "in the pages of Mr. Howells."

A published lecture by Walter Besant on *The Art of Fiction* was brought to James's attention especially by an article in the *Pall Mall Gazette* attacking his *An International Episode* for its psychological treatment as "fiction without adventure" and leaning upon Besant for support. This drew from James his famous essay "The Art of Fiction" in which be briefly makes his contemner ridiculous, calls the conception of the novel held by Dickens and Thackeray *naïf*, attacks Besant at certain points (especially on the score of "conscious moral purpose"), and then brilliantly expounds the theory he had advanced in "Alphonse Daudet"—that the purpose of the novel is to represent life. Robert Louis Stevenson, whom James had brought into the discussion, urbanely took up the gage in

"A Humble Remonstrance" but in an addendum leveled the sharpest attack on Howells to which he was subjected in the controversy:

> . . . none ever couched a lance with narrower convictions. His own work and those of his pupils and masters singly occupy his mind; he is the bondslave, the zealot of his school; he dreams of an advance in art like what there is in science; he thinks of past things as radically dead; he thinks a form can be outlived: a strange immersion in his own history; a stranger forgetfulness of the history of the race! Meanwhile by a glance at his own works . . . much of this illusion would be dispelled. For while he holds all the poor little orthodoxies of the day . . . the living quality of much that he has done is of a contrary . . . complexion. . . . A poet, a finished artist, . . . he has other passions than those he loves to draw. The obvious is not of necessity the normal; . . . and the danger is lest, in seeking to draw the normal, a man should draw the null. . . .

Though in part the Stevenson attack was retaliation for a deliberate snub by Howells, it was the first time a critic had separated Howells from James in the controversy, and James, concerned about the effect of that controversy on his own work in England, decided after reflection to take advantage of it. He had not at the moment any hope of diverting Howells from his battle with the English. Hence, he resolved to write an article on Howells which would plainly set forth such differences that two would no longer be considered one by the critics. He did this in a critical study in *Harper's Weekly* entitled "William Dean Howells," which ironically emphasized the narrow artistic convictions and all the poor little orthodoxies of the day to which Howells subscribed. He traced Howells's Anglophobia to his isolation in Venice during the Civil War when he had to put up with the London *Times* for news and with the talk of British tourists for conversation. He praised Mr. Howells's "unerring sentiment of the American character" while lamenting the impression a prospective visitor might get of American society from "the terrible practices at the country hotel in *Dr. Breen* and at the Boston boarding house in *A Woman's Reason*." He felt that Howells was "animated by a love of the common, the immediate, the familiar and vulgar elements of life."

> He thinks scarcely anything too paltry to be interesting, that the small and vulgar have been terribly neglected, and would rather see an exact account of a sentiment or character he stumbles against every day than a brilliant evocation of a passion or a type he has never seen and does not even particularly believe in.

James scoffed at novels in which "the only immoralities are aberrations of thought, like that of Silas Lapham, or excesses of beer, like that of Bartley Hubbard." He found Lapham's wife and Lemuel Barker's mate "exhaustive renderings of the type of virtue that worries." And he suggested, in conclusion, that style counted for less and less with Howells and that he appeared increasingly "to hold composition too cheap."

The attack must appear brutal even to the admirers of James, but it is not without parallel in other artistic careers and it was not wholly undeserved. Howells's reiterated proprietorship in James created an uncomfortable attachment and adversely affected James's fortunes. Further, it made James responsible for ideas he did not hold. Howells should have been forewarned by the differences with him that James freely expressed and by James's growing impatience with the tabus in English and American writing. On James's part a final motive might be found in a small desire to teach Howells that his criticism was not wholly "impressionistic!"

iii "Grow old along with me"

It is hard to believe that James did not think Howells might resent the devastating article in *Harper's Weekly* despite its thin sprinkling of praise. Howells had been dealt a heavy blow immediately after the Stevenson attack. So far as is known, however, he gave no visible sign of having felt either. There is no published letter between June 18, 1886, when the article appeared, and December 25, 1886, when Howells wrote James in part as follows:

Your most kind letter from Milan caused great excitement and rejoicing in this family. What could I ask more even if I had the cheek to ask half so much? One doesn't thank you for such a thing, I suppose, but I may tell you at least of my pride and pleasure in it. I'm disposed to make the most of the abundance of your kindness, for in many quarters here the book meets with little but misconceptions. If we regard it as nothing but an example of work in the new way—the performance of a man who won't and can't keep on doing what's been done already—its reception here by most of the reviews is extremely discouraging. . . . I find myself not really caring a great deal for the printed animosity, except as it means ignorance. I suspect it's an effect of the frankness about our civilization which you sometimes wondered I could practice with impunity. The impunity's gone now, I assure you.

Obviously James had written Howells in appreciation of one of the latter's novels; Mildred Howells, who equally obviously was not in possession of the conciliatory letter, surmises that the book was either *The Rise of Silas Lapham* or *The Minister's Charge*. It was the latter, and James's letter must have been in part a retraction, for he had censured each in *Harper's Weekly*. Howells's feeling that he had no right to ask what James had freely offered is based on his contrition for having involved James in controversy by his comparison of James's abilities with those of the great English novelists. Howells responded publicly to James's private overture with a wholly laudatory review of *The Princess Casamassima*—the most generous he had written up to that time—in the "Editor's Study" in *Harper's* in April, 1887: "We find *no* fault with Mr. Henry James's *Princess Casamassima*: it is a great novel; it is his greatest, and it is incomparably the greatest novel of the year in our language." Correspondence between the two novelists was resumed (though there are gaps in what has been published); but Howells, despite the experience that had jeopardized their friendship, continued to belabor the British in his columns and reviews. James was moved to mild protest at the beginning of 1888.

If we could have that rich conversation I should speak to you too of your monthly polemics in *Harper* and tell you . . . of certain parts of the business in which I am less with you than in others. It seems to me . . . you . . . sometimes make mistakes of proportion, and in general incline to insist more upon restrictions and limitations, the *a priori* formulas and interdictions, of our common art, than upon that priceless freedom which is to me the thing that makes it worth practising. . . . I am surprised sometimes, at the things you notice and seem to care about. One should move in a diviner air. . . .

How much Howells dwelt on "the *a priori* formulas and interdictions" may be judged from his *Criticism and Fiction*, gathered from the "Editor's Study" in 1891. But this book also goes beyond the article on James in its defamation of English writers, while lavish in its praise of James:

> . . . I value more such a novel as Mr. James's *Tragic Muse* than all the romantic attempts since Hawthorne. . . . To spin a yarn for the yarn's sake, that is an ideal worthy of a nineteenth-century Englishman . . . ; but wholly impossible to an American of Mr. Henry James's modernity. . . . To such a mind as his the story could never have value except as a means; it could not exist for him as an end; . . . it could be the frame, not possibly the picture.

But James did not take umbrage at this, for the better English reviewers and critics no longer lumped his work with that of Howells. In marking Howells off as fanatical, Stevenson had begun a process which was to culminate in the opinion of the *National Observer* in 1896 that "Mr. Howells' combativeness" had drawn on James quarrels he might otherwise have avoided. Along the way James's temperate and highly reflective "The Art of Fiction" had further helped in the separation, as had such a highly particularized attack as that in the *Speaker* in 1890 upon Howells, whom it characterized as "the great man who was to slay Dickens and Thackeray and to lead the children of Washington out of the Egyptian darkness of Romanticism." Attacks on James continued, to be sure; in fact, he was to complain bitterly of the reviewers, but there was less coupling of the names of Howells and James, and the latter's work was now more commonly censured in England for what were regarded as intrinsic faults.

Although the fine tribute to *The Princess* and the praise of *The Tragic Muse* may be taken as gestures of friendship and indications that all was forgiven, there is some evidence that James's treatment of him in *Harper's Weekly* still rankled slightly with Howells. In the series of articles in the *Ladies' Home Journal* which became *My Literary Passions* (1896), Howells, according James scant treatment, ambiguously observed, "I have my reserves in regard to certain things of his; if hard pressed I might undertake to better him here and there, but after I had done that I doubt, if I should like him so well." In Howells's *Literary Friends and Acquaintance* (1900) there is a pleasant recollection of Henry James, Sr., but no mention of his namesake. In his two-volume treatment of the *Heroines of Fiction*, where the reader might readily have expected some presentation of the great gallery of feminine types that James had created, Howells accords only a brief treatment to Daisy Miller. Further, Howells neglected to send James copies of his books, and James complained of the neglect. The fact that James purchased, from scant earnings, *Ragged Lady* (1898), "The Pursuit of the Piano," and "two or three other things" in order to read him "again as continuously as possible" may have somewhat mollified Howells's feelings. Howells sent him his next book of fiction, a collection of short stories, *A Pair of Patient Lovers* (1901). Thereafter the exchange of letters and of books was the regular practice of the two men.

But one great difference continued to exist between Howells and James, and the latter had pointed this up not only in his emphasis upon the "priceless freedom" of the novelist in his letter of remonstrance to Howells, but also in the *Harper's Weekly* attack. It is apparent that, to James, Howells was too reticent on the score of morals to be the emancipator of fiction he should have been. This much can be inferred from his remark on the wives of Lapham and Barker and from his observation that Howells preferred sentiment to passion. On May 17, 1890, James wrote Howells about *A Hazard of New Fortunes*, which he had just read, and stressed the limitation of this reticence:

> The *Hazard* is simply prodigious. . . . You are less *big* than Zola, but you are ever so much less clumsy and more really various, and moreover you and he don't see the same things. . . . there's a whole quarter of the heaven upon which . . . you seem consciously—is it consciously?—to have turned your back. . . .

When Howells was abroad again in 1897 James may have pointed up his thoughts on freedom in fiction to his friend, though much of their talk centered on practical ideas which Howells had for the marketing of James's work. It seems likely that James placed things in the *Cosmopolitan*, the *Chap Book*, *Collier's Weekly*, and the American edition of *Literature* at Howells's suggestion.

But the greatest service that Howells was to render James, beyond restoring his confidence, was to help him place *The Ambassadors* in the *North American Review*.

> My feelings don't permit me to wait to tell you that the communication I have just had from you surpasses for pure unadulterated charm any communication I have *ever* received. I am really quite overcome and weakened by your recital of the generous way in which you threw yourself into the scale of the arrangement, touching my so long unserialized serial, which is manifestly so excellent a thing for me. I had begun to despair of anything, when, abruptly, this brightens the view. For I *like*, extremely, the place the N.A.R. makes for my novel. . . . Charming to me also is the idea of your own beneficent paper in the same quarter—the complete detachment of which, however, from the current fiction itself I equally appreciate and applaud. . . .

Howells's "own beneficent paper," to which James alludes, was "Mr. Henry James's Later Work" printed in the *North American Review* in January, 1903, immediately before the first installment of *The Ambassadors*. In some ways this is the most remarkable document in the whole relationship between the two men. Howells had made in his *Criticism and Fiction* perhaps the most notorious justification for reticence in regard to illicit love in American fiction in the entire critical annals of the nineteenth century, arguing that authors and editors were compelled to reticence because a preponderance of the readers were young girls. He contended, further, that the manners of the novel had been steadily improving, and that the role of the novelist had become "something like that of a physician or priest . . . bound by laws as sacred as those of such professions." He felt that the critics who demanded "passion" had only the "passion of guilty love" in mind; he contended that it took more skill to develop other passions in the novel: grief, avarice, pity, ambition, hate, envy, devotion, and friendship. In his essay "Mr. Henry James's Later Work" he seems utterly and astonishingly to reverse himself. The bulk of the essay is a dialogue between Howells and an interlocutress to whom he assigns the today inadmissible point of view *which he himself had upheld* in *Criticism and Fiction:*

[She:] ". . . But do you think he ought to picture such life because it exists?"

"Do you find yourself much the worse for the *Wings of the Dove?*" I asked. "Or for *The Sacred Fount?* or for *The Awkward Age?* Or even for *What Maisie Knew?* They all picture much the same sort of life."

"Why, of course not. But it isn't so much what he says—he never says anything—but what he insinuates. I don't believe that is good for young girls."

"But if they don't know what it means? I'll allow that it isn't quite *jeune fille* in its implications, all of them; but maturity has its modest claims. Even in the interest of a knowledge of our mother-civilization, which is what Mr. James's insinuations impart, as I understand them."

"Well, young people cannot read him aloud together. You can't deny that."

"No, but elderly people can, and they are not to be ignored by the novelist always. I fancy the reader who brings some knowledge of good and evil, without being worse for it, to his work is the sort of reader Mr. James writes for. I can imagine him addressing himself to a circle of such readers as this *Review's* with a satisfaction, and a sense of liberation, which he might not feel in the following of the family magazines, and still not incriminate himself. I have heard a good deal said in reproach of the sort of life he portrays, in his later books; but I have not found his people of darker deeds or murkier motives than the average in fiction. I don't say, life."

"No certainly, so far as he tells you. It is what he *doesn't* tell that is so frightful. He leaves you to such awful conjectures. For instance, when Kate Croy——"

"When Kate Croy——?"

"No, I *won't* discuss it. But you know what I mean; and I don't believe there was ever such a girl."

"And you believe there was ever such a girl as Milly Theale?"

"Hundreds! She is true to the life. So perfectly American. . . .

Has Howells *completely* shifted his ground, as has just been assumed? No, the implication here seems to be that subject matter, like James's, is still unfit for the young girl, but she doesn't read the *North American Review* anyway; mature people do, and James is entitled to address them here on subjects excluded from "family" magazines, especially since he is treating English society. That is, we might be justified in assuming that Howells's attitude is permissive—he is solely bent on justifying the serialization of *The Ambassadors* in this particular review with its limited circulation. The fact that he finds James's people compelled by no "murkier motives" and committing no "darker deeds" than "the average in fiction" suggests that he was defending James in part from the strictures that had been laid on his morality the previous June by Frank Moore Colby and from the "reproaches" Howells had heard readers make. This raises the question: Is the whole dialogue a piece of self-defense, a justification of himself for having persuaded the *Review* to print *The Ambassadors*, in case the editors were attacked for it? Is the qualified retraction of his former well-known position, on the other hand, a possible limited surrender to James's argument for freedom for the novelist? Is it meant, in a word, as much for James as for the reader of the *Review* or for the general public? There is no clear answer to any of these questions because Howells's own position with regard to the proprieties is in no way clear. He wrote five novels after this, *The Son of Royal Langbrith* (1904), *Miss Bellard's Inspiration* (1905), *Fennel and Rue* (1908), *The Leatherwood God* (1916), and *The Vacation of the Kelwyns* (1920), which show no departure from his previous standards of reticence. Further, the "Gorki case" in 1905, in which Howells withdrew from the planned dinner to the Russian novelist because he was accompanied by his common law wife, displays a prudery as bad as anything recorded in Howells's youth. On the other hand, Howells accorded two sympathetic reviews and contributed an introduction to Stephen Crane's *Maggie* and was the first American editor to include a story by Theodore Dreiser in an anthology. The best that can be said would appear to be that Henry James's long protestation against his friend's narrowness succeeded in modifying Howells's attitude slightly towards the daring work of others but liberalized Howells's own compositions not a whit.

Although the influence of Henry James was negligible in diverting Howells from his "Victorian . . . preference of decency," Howells's attention to his friend and his solicitude for him increased as both their lives narrowed to a close. The record is one of continuous service: he acted as James's agent and he helped to prepare the way for James's visit to America in 1904. James visited Howells at his summer place in Kittery, Maine, and in Cambridge his feet had fallen into the old path of "shared literary secrets . . . , the dreams of youth, the titles of tales, the communities of friendship, the sympathies and patiences . . . of dear W. D. H.," hoping it would lead to its old terminus, Fresh Pond—only to find that extension of the "Park System" had practically swallowed the pond. There were other visits between the two men, but of their last meeting, there is no published record; Howells was in England in 1913 and in all likelihood saw his old friend then. In that year, he joined with T. S. Perry in discouraging some well-meaning fund raisers who meant to present James a gift for the purchase of furniture for Lamb House, since they knew how little James would care for such a gift. In 1910 he had contributed a letter, "One of the Public to the Author" to *The Henry James Year Book*, which pleased James much more. Howells said in part:

> After so many years ago your eager editor, and ever since your applausive critic, I ought not to feel bound to insist now upon my delight in the charms of your manner, the depth of your thought, the beauty of your art, which the grouping of these passages freshly witnesses even to such a veteran lover of your work as I; and in fact I do not feel so bound. I do not so much fulfill a duty as indulge a pleasure in owning my surprise at the constant succession of your felicities here.

In 1911 Howells led the effort in the United States and wrote the President of the Academy to attempt to secure the Nobel Prize for literature for Henry James; in 1915, though he expressed grief for "losing" James, he defended to Brander Matthews James's right to become a British citizen—and whimsically remarked that he himself was thinking of becoming a citizen of Maine. A month after James's death in 1916 he laid aside with relief an article on James when the contractor for it failed him, remanding his memories "to the past where I should have suffered so much in calling them up." Yet the last effort of his own life, undertaken before his fatal illness four years later but worked on after he was bedfast, was a review of *The Letters of Henry James* and the beginning of an article which was to be entitled "The American James." In their long lives, Howells and James had inflicted hurts on each other, but not more so than is common with persons closely associated, a fact which each seemed to appreciate, and their double striving, with Howells perhaps making the greater concessions, made it a path of amity at the end, as it was in the beginning.

AFTERWORD

To me, one of the most fascinating topics in the world is the relation of an author to his editor, for the latter may potentially assume a shaping or disciplinary attitude of advantage or disadvantage to the author. Some measure of the author's integrity as an artist is involved, particularly if the editor wishes alterations that affect the author's conception of his work. Too often critical examinations of these situations are rankly partisan, condemnatory of the editor out of hand. The pluralistic method demands a search into the motives and actions of both men, such as I have endeavored to employ here. In its original version the essay is heavily documented (dear God, 117 footnotes!) which the dubious reader may examine for the substantiality of the evidence. (I shall always fondly think of Henry Nash Smith who, at a memorable small dinner in New York, when I was assailed in friendly fashion from opposite sides by William M. Gibson and Leon Edel, closed the discussion with an abrupt, "But the evidence is all there!") I did not go into Howells' relationship to the publisher and the pressures exerted on him, if any, for Edward Harrison Cady had already supplied evidence as to Howells' general timidity, but perhaps I should have. Nevertheless, though no Maxwell Perkins, Howells was the best editor of his generation, far superior to T. B. Aldrich and others. After publication in *American Literature* this essay was translated into Japanese and circulated by the USIS through its cultural centers in Japan.

5   *THE TURN OF THE SCREW*
AND ALICE JAMES

THE TENDEREST of men, Henry James could hardly have used the illness of his sister Alice as the basis of a story while she lived, or later, without elaborately disguising it—particularly since that illness, though not concealed, was only guardedly revealed as mental. But the heroism of Alice, fully as much as his experience and special knowledge of hysteria, must have strongly tempted him to exploit the extraordinary dramatic possibilities of her disease long before he composed *The Turn of the Screw*. Delicacy, propriety, affection instantly inhibited the development of so rich a "germ," but it remained planted in James's ingenious and subtle mind until he could bring the derivative narrative forth so altered that his closest intimates would not suspect its source or connections. The product is one of the greatest horror stories of all time.

Until Edmund Wilson designated *The Turn of the Screw* a study in psychopathology, only three persons had the temerity to guess that it was something more than a ghost story—a view which still has the preponderance of support today. The three attracted no attention, but Wilson stirred up an indignant and vociferous opposition which literally "threw the book at him"—the book, however, being James's own comments on his story which could be read as leading away from Wilson's interpretation. It apparently did not occur to any of Wilson's critics that James might have an adequate motive for disguising his purpose in the tale; neither they nor Wilson referred to

Alice James, though her tragic story provides an explanation for the "ambiguity" of both the commentary and the tale itself. James's "strategy" consisted in overlaying his real story with another which might, with plausibility, be construed as a ghost story. The limitations of that "strategy" are, however, that it temporarily confounds the acute and perceptive and, like life, rewards the obtuse and conventional. Thanks to it, *The Turn of the Screw* continues to be misread as "a pure ghost story."

For a proper reading some of the difficulties that James himself interposed must be skirted or eliminated. The chief of these seems to be James's indication that the primary source of his inspiration was the fragment of a ghost story given him by a friend. A circle of intimates, one winter afternoon, round the hall fire of an old country house, lamenting the disappearance of the old-fashioned ghost story, were comforted by their host with "one of the scantest fragments of this form at its best," got from a lady when he was young:

> The story would have been thrilling could she have found herself in better possession of it, dealing as it did with a couple of small children in an out-of-the-way place, to whom the spirits of certain bad servants, dead in the employ of the house, were believed to have appeared with the design of "getting hold" of them. This was all, but there had been more, which my old friend's converser had lost the thread of: she could only assure him of the wonder of the allegations as she had anciently heard them made.

When James's letters were published in 1920, the novelist's recollection of this "germ" for his tale was apparently supported by a letter to Arthur Christopher Benson, dated 11 March 1898, after the story had begun to appear in *Collier's Weekly*, in which the host is stated to have been the latter's distinguished father, the Archbishop, and the time and place "one of those two memorable—never to be obliterated—winter nights that I spent at the sweet Addington . . . in the drawing room by the fire." The "essence" of the anecdote struck James and he went home and made a note of it "of the most scrappy kind." With the publication of James's *Notebooks* (1947) his "scrappy" memorandum came to light:

> *Saturday, January 12th, 1895.* Note here the ghost-story told me at Addington (evening of Thursday 10th), by the Archbishop of Canterbury: the mere vague, undetailed faint sketch of it—being all that he had been told (very badly and imperfectly), by a lady who had no art of relation, and no clearness: the story of the young children (indefinite number and age) left to the care of the servants in an old country house, through the death, presumably, of the parents. The servants, wicked and depraved, corrupt and deprave the children; the children are bad, full of evil, to a sinister degree. The servants *die* (the story vague about the way of it) and their apparitions, figures, return to haunt the house *and* children, to whom they seem to beckon, whom they invite and solicit, from across dangerous places, the deep ditch of a sunk fence, etc.—so that the children may destroy themselves, by responding, by getting into their power. So long as the children are kept from them, they are not lost; but they try and try and try, these evil presences, to get hold of them. It is a question of the children "coming over to where they are." It is all obscure and imperfect, the picture, the story, but there is a suggestion of a strangely gruesome effect in it. The story to be told—tolerably obviously—by an outside spectator, observer.

Yet this double verification of the source of his tale is undermined as absolute by the complete double failure of A. C. Benson and his brother to recall that their father ever told such a story. In fact, they are unusually emphatic in their separate denials that the tale was in their father's repertoire. This contradiction is extraordinary, but it is still more extraordinary that James tries immediately, in fact almost insistently, to establish his indebtedness to the Archbishop, for it was not his habit thus to acknowledge his sources. May he not have had a special reason for it in this instance?

Leaving this question unanswered for the moment and temporarily admitting that the Archbishop's narrative may have been in some degree a source, let us concentrate our

attention on the most important element that the anecdote leaves out—the narrator of the tale. James's memorandum merely indicates that he once felt that the narrator
should be "an outside spectator," an objective observer.
This objective narrator he has supplied in the "I"-reporter
of the Prologue to the tale, but in addition the Prologue
contains *three* other narrators—an extraordinary circum-
stance, surely, in the work of a writer famous for economy
of means. The first of this triumvirate of story tellers is a
man named Griffin who has finished his yarn just before
the Prologue opens. It was a tale of "an appearance, of a
dreadful kind, to a little boy sleeping in a room with his
mother and waking her not to dissipate his dread and
soothe him to sleep again, but to encounter also, herself,
before she had succeeded in doing so, the same sight that
had shaken him." A griffin, of course, is a fanciful beast,
and we have every reason to believe that Griffin has told a
supernatural story with a genuine apparition in it, an
apparition which frightens a child and its parent. Only one
of Griffin's auditors challenges this interpretation; this is
Douglas, the second narrator, who is to produce the
written narrative of the governess and the two terrified
children. Douglas is obviously named after that noble Scot
in Henry IV, Part I, famous for his candor, so faithful in a
bad cause, unmasking two pretenders before he discovers
the King, that after his capture he is set free by Prince Hal.
Foil to Griffin, Douglas demurs, "I quite agree—in regard
to Griffin's ghost, *or whatever it was*—that its appearing
first to the little boy . . . adds a particular touch" (my
italics). That sharp phrase, *"or whatever it was,"* betrays
Douglas' skepticism in regard to supernatural appearances
and all but pledges—does it not?—that the tale which he
produces, while it will "for sheer terror" surpass everything, will *not* deal with apparitions. Douglas is not a true
narrator, but the reader of, and minor commentator on, a
long autobiographical document entrusted to him some
twenty years ago by his younger sister's governess, who is
the last and chief narrator of *The Turn of the Screw*.
Douglas vouches with such fervor for the good character of
the governess that his friends properly suspect him of

having been deeply in love with her. A suggestion that she may have reciprocated his emotion lies in the fact that, in the face of death, she turned over to him her personal account of a truly harrowing experience which led to the death of one of her charges, for which in some degree she may have been held responsible. May not the relation of these two, of Douglas and the governess, somewhat neglected by the critics, be important for a full understanding of *The Turn of the Screw?*

The fact that they have lacked Douglas' faith in the governess and have been struck by her facility for involvement (she falls in love with her handsome employer on sight has induced a few critics to inquire into her role and into the meaning of her narrative. The first to do this was the anonymous reviewer in the *Critic*, who, shortly after the story appeared in book form, observed, "the heroine . . . has nothing in the least substantial upon which to base her deep and startling cognitions. She perceives what is beyond perception, and the reader who begins by questioning whether she is supposed to be sane ends by accepting her conclusions and thrilling over the horrors they involve." In 1919 Professor Henry A. Beers casually observed in an essay on Hawthorne: "Recall the ghosts in Henry James's *The Turn of the Screw*—just a suspicion of evil presences. The true interpretation of that story I have sometimes thought to be, that the woman who saw the phantoms was mad."

Five years later, Miss Edna Kenton, noting that James had described the tale as "a piece of ingenuity, pure and simple, of cold artistic calculation, an *amusette* to catch those not easily caught," indicated that she thought *The Turn of the Screw* to be a kind of hoax story to test the attentiveness of his readers, the lazy apprehending it only as a ghost story, the most attentive getting a deeper richness. It is the Kenton thesis that the ghosts *and the children*, the pictorial isolation, are "only the exquisite dramatizations of her [the governess'] little personal mystery, figures for the ebb and flow of the troubled thought within her mind, acting out her story."

Tacitly avoiding Miss Kenton's hoax thesis but fully

acknowledging the generic power of her suggestion in regard to the character of the governess, Edmund Wilson in a now famous and always challenging article, "The Ambiguity of Henry James," in the Henry James issue of *Hound & Horn,* contended that the key to *The Turn of the Screw* lies in the fact that "the governess who is made to tell the story is a neurotic case of sex repression, and that the ghosts are not real ghosts but hallucinations of the governess." In 1938 and again in 1948 Wilson, as a result of his own reading and reflection, revised his case, but stuck with conviction to his major premise, the neuroticism of the governess. She is still the fluttered, anxious girl out of a Hampshire vicarage who in her first interview becomes infatuated with her employer, and after confused thinking about him at Bly, discovers her first apparition, the figure of a man on a tower. With her help the figure, after a second appearance, is identified by the housekeeper, Mrs. Grose, as that of the master's handsome valet Peter Quint (now dead), who had appropriated the master's clothes and used "to play with the little boy [Miles] . . . to spoil him." By the shore of a lake where she is watching the little girl Flora at play, the governess sees another apparition, that of Miss Jessel her predecessor, who allegedly had had an affair with the valet. Suspecting the children as privy to this relationship, she is confirmed in her notion that they have been previously corrupted by these evil servants who have come back to get them. The game of protection which she plays is, however, according to Wilson's further analysis, one in which she transfers her own terror, and *more,* to the children, thwarts the boy's desire to re-enter school or to write to his uncle, fixes upon him an unnatural fervid affection, and finally alienates the housekeeper before she literally frightens her young male charge to death.

Like Miss Kenton, Wilson insists that nobody but the governess sees the ghosts. "She believes that the children see them, but there is never any proof that they do. The housekeeper insists that she does not see them; it is apparently the governess who frightens her." At only one point was Wilson's interpretation labored; he could not adequately explain how Mrs. Grose was able to identify the male apparition from the description given by the governess (who had never met the deceased valet) after her second encounter. The critics of the Wilson thesis—and they were an insistent score—bore down so heavily on this weakness that in 1948 Wilson capitulated, adding a separate note of retraction to his essay: "It is quite plain that James's conscious intention . . . was to write a *bona fide* ghost story; . . . not merely is the governess self-deceived but . . . James is self-deceived about her."

ii

That James could be so completely deceived about the motivation of any one of his characters is a thesis very hard to accept in view of his marvelous understanding of human psychology; hence a reasonable doubt bids us review the whole difficulty again. The identification of Peter Quint by the housekeeper is at present the seemingly insurmountable thing, and here we must note that the governess herself indicates to Mrs. Grose, when the latter wavers in accepting the young woman's version of the extraordinary events, that it is *the unimpeachable proof* that she has *not* invented the apparitions: "To hold her [Mrs. Grose] perfectly . . . I found I had only to ask her how, if I had 'made it up,' I came to be able to give, of each of the persons appearing to me, a picture disclosing, to the last detail, their special marks—a portrait on exhibition of which she had instantly recognized and named them." If we continue to persist in thinking this a crushing demonstration that the apparitions are supernatural, are we not more gullible than Mrs. Grose, who at least became suspicious enough, toward the end of the tale, to separate little Flora from the governess and thus save her life?

Mrs. Grose and we are the victims of a palpable deception, the trick of a demonstrable, pathological liar, a pitiful but dangerous person, with an unhinged fancy. We cannot examine all of the minute details of the governess' tendency (to the close reader they are multitudinous), but we can glance at one or two of the larger demonstrations of her complete unreliability. At the climax of the tale the governess promises to write a letter to her employer telling him of the state of things at Bly; this letter is stolen by suspicious little Miles, who opens it to discover, as he confesses and as she herself reiterates, that it contains "nothing." Again, in the sixteeenth chapter, the governess reports to Mrs. Grose a conversation which she asserts she has just had with the "ghost" of Miss Jessel in which the latter admitted she is "of the lost" and "of the damned" and that she "wants Flora." But we ourselves have just witnessed through the governess' eyes the whole of that encounter and the only words uttered were by the governess, —" 'You terrible, miserable woman!' . . . *There was nothing in the room the next minute but the sunshine* [italics, mine]. . . ." And finally, let us look closely at the first appearance of the apparition of Miss Jessel, the former governess. The present governess is seated before a little lake and Flora is at play in front of her; she suddenly becomes aware "without direct vision" of "the presence, at a distance of a third person." Lifting her eyes from her sewing, the governess perceives a specter across the lake, but little Flora, busy at fitting one piece of wood into another to form a boat, is *"back to* the water" [italics mine] and obviously does not see the alleged visitant. Yet when the governess reports the episode to Mrs. Grose, she states a flat untruth, "Flora *saw!"* Upon the housekeeper's expressing some doubt about the episode, the governess breaks out with, "Then ask Flora—*she's* sure!" But she instantly apprehends the danger from this and adds, in consternation, "No, for God's sake, *don't!* . . . she'll lie!" If this is a genuine ghost story, are not the governess' lies inexplicable? Must we not trust her completely to accept the presences as ghosts and not hallucinations?

With some knowledge now of the governess' state, we may look at the mystery of the identification of Peter Quint. After her *second* encounter with the male apparition, the governess produces some minute details about his appearance: he was hatless, wore smart clothes (not his own), had curly red hair and little whiskers. He might have been an actor, but he was never a gentleman. Mrs. Grose (who, the governess sees, has already recognized the man) asks if he were handsome. " 'Remarkably!' . . . She had faltered but a second. 'Quint!' she cried . . . 'Peter Quint, his valet, when he was here!' " The housekeeper has come out with the identification that the governess *expected*.

When the governess came to Bly, she knew only, on the word of her employer, that her predecessor, Miss Jessel, "was a most respectable person." During her second day at Bly she is conducted about the place by little Flora, who shows it to her "room by room, *secret by secret, displaying a disposition to tell me so many more things than she was asked* [italics mine]." This innocent loquacious trait in little Flora must be kept in mind. Two days later the governess picks up from the housekeeper the fact that there had been a man around who had an eye for "young pretty" women, like Miss Jessel and the present governess. This sets her excitable mind at work, and, after she has had her first hallucination, from the prattle of her youngest charge, from her own seemingly artless prompting of the children, and finally from a trip of inquiry to the village, as John Silver has shown, she constructs the detailed description which she supplies to Mrs. Grose in reporting the second visitation. This is Silver's proof (the housekeeper speaks first):

> "Was he a gentleman?"
> I found I had no need to think. "No." . . .
> "Then nobody about the place? *Nobody from the village?*"
> "Nobody—nobody. *I didn't tell you, but I made sure.*"

It is important to note also that the governess exhibits during her adventure at Bly a mind singularly susceptible to evil suggestion. The letter informing her that Miles has been dismissed from school gives no reason; since he had been admitted on trial, being much younger than any of his fellows, the normal assumption would be that it hadn't worked out. But the governess jumps to the preposterous conclusion in regard to the child (he's only ten!) "he's an injury to others." A little later, on no evidence whatsoever, she thinks of "the little, horrid, unclean school-world" from which Miles was dismissed. Similarly, there is absolutely no reason for supposing the former governess and valet corrupt; the master gives Miss Jessel a good character and Quint had been his trusted personal man-servant. It is Mrs. Grose, out of a petty jealousy common to domestic servants, who, at the prompting of the governess, embroiders the tale about a relation between the pair; it is the governess who gobbles up every morsel of this and invents the theme of their evil designs upon the children. That she carries her insinuations to the children themselves (despite what she says to the contrary) is indicated by Mrs. Grose's declaration, after she had taken over Flora, that she has heard "horrors" from the artless child. How can those who believe that this is a ghost story justify her impulse, when she perceives Miles is afraid of her, to make him really fear? Miles betrays that she has suggested an evil relationship between him and Quint, for when in the last scene she calls his direct attention to her specter (Miles "glaring vainly over the place and missing wholly"), the boy guesses at what she means him to see and names her a fiend: "Peter Quint—you devil!"

Fiend she is, but a sick young woman, too. It is a triumph of James's art that he can give so much pathological information about the governess without damaging her credibility for many readers. He shows her apprehensive about going to Bly (she has altogether four sleepless nights during the transition), yet her susceptibility to masculine charm is such that she pushes aside her fears to go as a result of her effortless conquest by the master; to the end of her tale her sudden neurotic infatuation is the mainspring of her action—she seeks to wring an admission from the tortured boy in order to clear herself with his handsome uncle. She sequesters the children's letters because "they were too beautiful to be posted; I kept them myself; I have them to this hour." The governess will not herself write about events at Bly because she fears that the master will look upon her letter as a subtle device "to attract his attention to my slighted charms." From the beginning to the end she reiterates that she is highly disturbed, excited, and in a nervous state. She is, in addition, "in receipt these days of disturbing letters from home, where things are not going well." There is a broad hint that her trouble is hereditary—she speaks unguardedly of "the eccentric nature of my father." She exults in her superiority to Mrs. Grose and in the way in which she can influence that ignorant woman: "I had made her the receptacle of lurid things, but there was an odd recognition of my superiority. . . . She offered her mind to my disclosures as, had I wished to mix a witch's broth and proposed it with assurance, she would have held out a large clean saucepan." With quite disarming candor, the governess summarizes herself, "I was queer company enough—quite as queer as the company I received"— meaning her hallucinated visitors. James with marvelous irony, perhaps the best example in his fiction, has the mad young woman run around the house to a window where she has just seen a visitant and peer in herself—to frighten Mrs. Grose half out of her wits; then the novelist caps it with the governess' observation, "I wondered why *she* should be scared." Does James not give the whole ingenious game away when, after one frightening episode, he has the little boy quiet the governess by playing the piano, and she thinks, "David playing to Saul could never have shown a finer sense of the occasion"? Saul was possessed of an evil spirit when the youth was sent for, and "David took an harp, and played with his hand; so Saul was refreshed, and was well, and the evil spirit departed from him" (I Samuel, 16: 14–23).

iii

One thing is clear, if James got his anecdote from Archbishop Benson, he did not mean us to take it as the *only* source of his story. He specifically labels it "the private source." Might there not have been public sources, i.e., things in print, available to everyone? Has it been properly noticed that James confesses to *many* "intellectual echoes" in recalling the creation of the tale? He adds further, "To knead the subject of my young friend's, the supposititious narrator's mystification thick . . . I seem to see draw behind it today a train of associations . . . so numerous I can but pick among them for reference." Not all of these possibilities can be investigated here, but one of them can hardly be neglected—the direct influence of Sigmund Freud.

Wilson's provocative paper should have led the author or others to the writings of Freud for a source for *The Turn of the Screw*. While most critics would concede that an author of genius could in his characterizations anticipate a later scientific elucidation of behavior, none has held that James in his study of the governess combined the perceptions of genius with some actual technical knowledge. The date of the story, 1898, seems too early, save for the remote possibility that there might be something relevant in that early publication of Doctors Breuer and Freud—*Studien über Hysterie*—in 1895. But indeed here *is* included a case of the greatest relevancy, one which supplies more important elements than Archbishop Benson's anecdote, "The Case of Miss Lucy R."

A victim of "chronic purulent rhinitis," Lucy R. came to Freud late in 1891 for a treatment that lasted nine weeks and resulted in a complete cure. Lucy R. was the governess of two children, the daughters of a factory superintendent living in the suburbs of Vienna. She was "an English lady of rather delicate constitution" who was suffering from "depression and lassitude" as well as being "tormented by the subjective sensations of smell," especially the smell of burned pastry. Freud's inquiry led to the discovery that this odor was associated with an actual culinary disaster which had occurred two days prior to her birthday when Lucy R. was teaching her charges to cook in the schoolroom. A letter had arrived from her mother in Glasgow which the children had seized and kept from her (to retain for her birthday) and during the friendly scuffle the cooking had been forgotten. Struck by the fact that the governess' illness had been produced by so small an event, Freud pressed further to discover that she was thinking of returning to her mother, who, he developed, stood in no need of her. The governess then confessed that the house had become "unbearable" to her. "The housekeeper, the cook, and the French maid seemed to be under the impression that I was too proud for my position. They united in intriguing against me and told the grandfather of the children all sorts of things about me." She complained to the grandfather and the father; not receiving, however, quite the support she expected, she offered her resignation, but was persuaded by the father to remain. It was in this period of crisis that the schoolroom accident occurred.

Though Freud had now an adequate "analysis of the subjective sensation of smell," he still was not satisfied, and he made a bold suggestion to the governess in order to study its effect:

> I told her I did not believe all these things [exceptional "attachment for the children and sensitiveness towards other persons of the household"] were simply due to her affection for the children, but that I thought she was rather in love with the master, perhaps unwittingly, that she really nurtured the hope of taking the place of the [dead] mother, and it was for that reason that she became so sensitive to the servants. . . . She feared lest they would scoff at her. She answered in her laconic manner: "Yes, I believe it is so."—"But if you knew you were in love with the master, why did you not tell me so?"—"But I did not know it, or rather I did not wish to know it. I wished to crowd it out of my mind."

The governess was not ashamed because she loved the man, she told Freud; she feared ridicule if her feelings were discovered, for he was rich, of a prominent family, and her employer. After this admission she readily gave a complete account of her infatuation: *Her love had sprung out of a single intimate interview with the master.* "He became milder and much more cordial than usual, he told her how much he counted on her in the bringing up of his children, and looked at her rather peculiarly. It was at this moment that she began to love him, and gladly occupied herself with the pleasing hopes she conceived during that conversation. However, this was not followed by anything else, and despite her waiting and persevering, no other heart-to-heart talk following, she decided to crowd it out of her mind."

The governess' confession led to a strange symbolic substitution in her subjective sense of smell—that of the aroma of a cigar; Freud determined by analysis to remove this new memory symbol and thus get at the real root of the neurosis. A visitor, an elderly accountant, after dinner when the men were smoking, had kissed the children and thrown the father into a rage. This recalled an earlier scene in which a lady visitor had also kissed both children on the lips; the father had barely controlled himself until she was gone and then had berated the unfortunate governess. "He said that he held her responsible for this kissing . . . that if it ever happened again, he would trust the education of his children to someone else. This occurred while she believed herself loved and waited for a repetition of that serious and friendly talk. This episode shattered all her hopes." Miss Lucy R. having thus completely disburdened her memory, her rhinitis and neurosis were cured and her sense of smell was restored.

There is one over-all resemblance between "The Case of Miss Lucy R." and the story of the governess of Bly: they are both presented as reports or case histories, within a frame, for unlike most of James's stories, *The Turn of the Screw* is a tale with an elaborate portico. As we have seen, a man named Douglas produces a document which is the governess' story. It is Douglas who tells us that the governess began her adventure by falling in love in the single interview that she had with her future employer—as did Lucy R. This instant infatuation, decidedly not typical of James's stories, may be taken as a sign of susceptibility or abnormality. The employer is rich and handsome and of an old Essex family; he is the uncle of orphaned chil-

dren—not two girls, but a niece and a nephew—whom he
has neither the experience nor the patience to minister to
personally. Like Miss Lucy's master, this new master gives
the governess a sense of commission and trust in the
interview, a factor in her infatuation.

And as for the governess' "case"—the story within the
story of *The Turn of the Screw*—that has special points of
resemblance also with "The Case of Miss Lucy R." The
valet and the former governess may be seen as trying to
possess little Miles and Flora in their protectress' disturbed
fancy as did the kissing male and female visitors the
children of the Vienna manufacturer—hint enough for
James to differentiate the sexless "bad servants" of Archbishop Benson's anecdote. In the episode of the children's
retaining Miss Lucy's letter at a crucial time may well be
the germ of the whole elaborate business with letters in
The Turn of the Screw: the governess retains a letter from
Miles's school saying his return is not desired, she prevents
Mrs. Grose from engaging to get a letter written to the
master describing conditions at Bly, and the empty letter
which she herself prepares and which is stolen and
destroyed by Miles.

In Miss Lucy's fear that others would discern her
feelings is the governess' dread that Miles will reveal them
to his uncle and a hint of the horrified suspicion with
which the other servants at Bly regard her after Mrs.
Grose departs with the ill little Flora for London—thereby
saving certainly the child's mind, if not her life. On
the other hand, the governess early reveals her love for the
master to Mrs. Grose with much the same candor that
had surprised Freud in Lucy R. Whether James was
influenced by Freud's analysis of Lucy's difficulties with
her sense of smell or not, his governess has a peculiarly
keen organ—she notes the smell of lately baked bread in
the housekeeper's living room, the "fragrance and purity
about the children," and even the frightened talk
of little Miles, just before his death, comes to her "like a
waft of fragrance." The impatience of the children's
bachelor uncle (which the governess seems to dread

throughout her adventure) derives from the impetuosity
of the Vienna manufacturer as certainly as the governess'
characterization as a rural parson's daughter comes from
the Glasgow mother of Miss Lucy, a suggestion redolent of
Presbyterianism.

⌣ Most important of all, James's governess experiences
what Freud defines as a traumatic experience—similar to
the rebuke of Miss Lucy—shortly after coming to Bly.
After accepting the post with both trepidation and hope,
she passes two sleepless nights in London, is possessed by
anxiety on her way down to Bly, is unable to sleep the first
night there, and then has a "second [really a fourth]
sleepless night." While she is in this exhausted condition,
she receives from her employer an unopened letter which
announces Miles's dismissal from school. But the unopened letter reveals to her not merely her employer's
indifference to the orphans in her care but to herself. Like
the reproof given to Lucy R., it shatters her hope of some
sort of intimacy with her employer, and the shock of that
experience produces from her the senseless traumatic
charges against little Miles. Finally, we are given the
broadest possible hint that the governess is ill, for her all
important interview takes place in "Harley Street"—the
conventional "physicians' row" of London. Thus, like T. S.
Eliot, James has provided us with a sort of "objective
correlative" for reading the story.

Seemingly the most difficult evaluation of the governess
to accept is that supplied through Douglas, who produces
her case and who reports later, when he knew her, "She
was a most charming person . . . ," and reiterates, "She
was the most agreeable woman I have ever known in her
position; she would have been worthy of any whatever." It
is further obvious that he had been in love with her when
she was his younger sister's governess—without knowing
of her illness which had obviously passed. Indeed, she is so
attractive as Henry James presents her—the courageous
protectress in her own mind to the children whom she
betrays—that the majority of critics are unwilling to
suspect any wrong of her. But she herself had realized the

danger of a recurrence of her madness, and when Douglas had urged marriage upon her and she had repeatedly refused, she had resolved upon writing out the history of her aberration in order that *he* might understand. Is not this the most plausible explanation to account for his possession of the narrative? She did not want him to think her merely capriciously cruel. This explanation has the merit, at least, of giving to *The Turn of the Screw* its final artistic unity, for when it is made, what we have called the "portico" or "Prologue" to the tale becomes its climax and the governess is translated into the heroine whom everyone apparently wants her to be.

iv

Despite this interpretation of *The Turn of the Screw*, some may claim that, though "The Case of Miss Lucy R." was available, it would hardly have come to James's knowledge. This brings us to the tragic story of Alice James, as revealed in her *Journal*. This woman, of whom the novelist was so fond, lucid and brilliant most of the time, was subject to "violent turns of hysteria," the first attacks occurring in 1867 or 1868 (or earlier), when she was nearing twenty. She writes of her struggle to conquer these "turns":

> As I used to sit immovable, reading in the library, with waves of violent inclination suddenly invading my muscles, taking some one of their varied forms, such as throwing myself out the window or knocking off the head of the benignant Pater, as he sat, with his silver locks, writing at his table; it used to seem to me that the only difference between me and the insane was that I had all the horrors and suffering of insanity, but the duties of doctor, nurse, and strait jacket imposed on me too.

One of her worst attacks came in the "hideous summer of 1876 when I went down to the deep sea and its waters closed over me and I knew neither hope nor peace." "Her malady is a kind of which little is known," her mother reports sadly, and from family letters we learn that "Alice is in New York undergoing motorpathy with Dr. Taylor" or "is being treated electrically by Dr. Neftel." The Monro treatment is tried and abandoned. After the death of her mother ("Alice is unaccountably upheld after this blow," her brother Robertson writes) and that of her father, she went to England to be where her brother Henry could care for her. London came to be regarded as too taxing, and she was located with a companion, Kate Loring, in Bournemouth, and then, when she was "much less well," in Leamington. During her English illnesses she was attended by various distinguished alienists; but in December 1891 she was subjected, at the suggestion of William James, to the "therapeutic possibilities" of hypnotism as a device to relieve "all hideous nervous distresses" and pain, which morphine could not.

This treatment of hysteria had been utilized by the great French doctor J.-M. Charcot. In 1882 William James had studied with Charcot and the following year Alphonse Daudet, Henry's friend, had dedicated a novel, *L'Evangeliste*, to Charcot. Henry had used the novel for suggestions for *The Bostonians*, his neurotic Olive Chancellor apparently being derived from Daudet's neurotic Mme Autheman, and both in turn from the studies of Charcot. Hence there is no reason to suppose that Henry James was not as well acquainted with Charcot's therapy as was his brother William. And is it not reasonable to suppose that, when the methods of the Frenchman were succeeded by those of Breuer and Freud, Henry James became acquainted with those as well? If he did not come to read *Studien über Hysterie* because of his continuing interest in his sister's case (she had died of cancer and other complications on 6 March 1892), it is possible that F. W. H. Myers, who had written the first notice of the book in English, may have brought it to his attention. But is it not easier to suppose, in view of their common interest in the nervous illness of their deceased sister, that William James may have called *Studien über Hysterie* to the attention of Henry sometime between 1895 and 1898? In one of his Lowell lectures in 1896 William had declared, "In the relief of certain hysterias by handling the buried idea, whether as in Freud or Janet, we see a portent of the possible usefulness of these discoveries. The awful becomes relatively trivial." In his second lecture on "Conversion" in the Gifford lectures of 1901–02 at Edinburgh, William praised "the wonderful explorations by . . . Janet, Breuer, Freud, . . . and others of the subliminal consciousness of patients with hysteria." While it is true that William came to suspect Freud, almost a decade later, as "a man obsessed with fixed ideas," in the time prior to his brother's composition of *The Turn of the Screw* it would seem that he was most favorably disposed toward the Vienna psychiatrist.

But prior to any knowledge of *Studien über Hysterie* was Henry James's personal acquaintance, of course, with the illness of his sister and with the delusions and fantasies of that illness. "Henry, the Patient, I should call him," Alice had paid him tribute in her *Journal*. "I have given him endless care and anxiety, but notwithstanding this and the fantastic nature of my troubles, I have never seen an impatient look on his face. . . . He comes at my slightest sign, and 'hangs on' to whatever organ may be in eruption, and gives me calm and solace by assuring me my nerves are his nerves, and my stomach his stomach." When William suggested hypnosis as a measure to relieve pain in Alice's last illness, Henry assented to the treatment though the practitioner, Dr. Charles Lloyd Tuckey, was the pioneer in England. About a year after Alice's death, the novelist wrote of Doctor Hugh in "The Middle Years," "This young friend, for a representative of the new psychology, was himself easily hypnotised, and if he became abnormally communicative it was only a sign of his real subjection." When Alice's *Journal* came into Henry's hands, he was "immensely impressed with the thing as a revelation of a moral . . . picture. It is heroic in its individuality, its independence—its face-to-face with the universe for and by herself." In the fortitude of Alice James facing her destiny James may have got the inspiration for making the governess the heroine of his tale and the confessor of her own terrible burden to her lover. But he noted other things in Alice's *Journal*: her lively curiosity for sexual anecdotes, such as the premarital chastity of her previous doctor, Sir Andrew Clark, and the vices of the Eton boys. When she sets down as fact Kate Loring's *always* coming, at a turn of the stairs, upon a waiter and a chambermaid, in "osculatory relaxations," Henry could have regarded that as a shared fantasy, but it may have suggested to him the relations of Peter Quint and Miss Jessel as imagined by the governess. One of the tiniest hints in Alice's *Journal* may be seen as richly fertile in relation to *The Turn of the Screw*: Alice notes, "I can't read anything suggestive, or that survives, or links itself to experience, for it sets my silly stomach fluttering, and my flimsy head skipping so that I have to stop." The governess had been reading Fielding's *Amelia* with great excitement (it having been denied her at home) at a "horribly late" hour when she becomes aware of "something undefinably astir in the house"; she hastily rises, has an hallucination of Quint on the stair, and later sees little Miles on the lawn staring up at—she assumes—Quint on the tower, but really up at his sister Flora. Now the pertinence of the forbidden book is this: because her husband is frequently cast into prison, the beautiful Amelia, pursued by two ardent would-be seducers through a series of exciting adventures, is the sole protectress of two little children, a boy and a girl, Billy being "a good soldier-like Christian." James put *Amelia* into the governess' hands because she could identify with the heroine: Amelia suffers early in the novel from what "some call a fever on the spirits, some a nervous fever, some the vapours, and some the hysterics," but which her husband pronounces "a sort of complication of all the diseases together, with almost madness added to them." James's own interest in *Amelia* was probably aroused because one of the tenacious seducers was named "Colonel James" whereas the other remains unnamed throughout and is simply referred to as "the noble peer." When Douglas of *The Turn of the Screw* fails to reveal the name of the governess, that might be regarded as the protection a lover might offer, but the failure of Mrs.

Grose or anyone else ever to call the governess by name, suggested by Fielding's omission possibly, can only be looked upon as an unconscious revelation of how deeply fixed was James's caution to avoid suspicion that his narrative had its source in Alice's illness.

James's dependence on his personal knowledge of hysteria and on "The Case of Miss Lucy R." makes it clear that Miss Kenton and Edmund Wilson were profoundly right in their characterization of the governess: there are no "ghosts" in the story—the phantoms are creations of an hysterical mind, they are hallucinations. Miss Kenton and Wilson, however, neglect the befuddled heroism of the girl's role. Just how much of the governess' narrative James meant as fantasy may be difficult to determine: Wilson accepts the children as real and the death of little Miles as a fact; Miss Kenton suggests that even the children— "what they are and what they do—are only exquisite dramatizations of her [the governess'] little personal mystery, figures for the ebb and flow of troubled thought within her mind, acting out her story." If Miss Kenton is right, there is no tragedy in *The Turn of the Screw*. There is only ill-health. But this interpretation is not consistent with James's declaration to Dr. Louis Waldstein, "But, ah, the exposure indeed, the helpless plasticity that isn't dear or sacred to somebody! That was my little tragedy . . ."; or his confession to F. W. H. Myers, "The thing . . . I most wanted not to fail of doing . . . was to give the impression of the communication to the children of the most infernal imaginable evil and danger—the condition, on their part, of being as *exposed* as we can humanly conceive children to be."

If there are things in the Preface to the volume containing *The Turn of the Screw*, or elsewhere, that suggest something short of tragedy for both children *and the governess*, or are ambiguous or mystifying, they are justifiably so: James had the duty of shielding Alice's memory—which he did in such artless phrases as "my bogey-tale," my "irresponsible little fiction," my "fairy tale pure and simple," behind which he could hide all that he wished to hide. Perhaps even ascribing the main source of the story to Archbishop Benson whose anecdote embodied ghosts was also an effort to disguise the truth in the tale. Should we not wonder, perhaps, that James did not more positively emphasize the possibilities of reading the tale as a ghost story, did not further lead the reader astray, save that there must have been a faint hope lodged in his heart that the central motif in his story, the horror of children betrayed by their protectress, an innocent mad woman, who, in her turn, becomes heroic, might in a long time emerge and his transcendent skill as an artist be understood? *The Turn of the Screw* is at once the most horrific and tender tale of the nineteenth century. "There is no excellent beauty," said Lord Bacon, "that hath not some strangeness in the proportion."

AFTERWORD

Had I not determined upon a chronological arrangement for the pieces in this volume, I would have placed this essay last, for, with my treatment elsewhere of *The Princess Casamassima, The Ambassadors,* and *The Golden Bowl,* it represents the best I can probably do with the pluralistic approach. I have brought into play as many different methods as I then thought possible to produce what I hope will be ultimately a viable interpretation of *The Turn of the Screw.* Toward the close of much work upon the essay, however, I discovered parallels between *Villette* by Charlotte Brontë and the tale. Borrowings from *Jane Eyre* had already been noted and Lionel Stevenson had called my attention to structural similarities in *Wuthering Heights.* Knowing that Clement Shorter, an editor new to Henry James, had published *The Other House,* which is also a story of the murder of a child, I surmised that James intended this story also for Shorter and *The Illustrated London News* and delved into the work of the Brontës to discover Shorter's taste since the latter had just published *Charlotte Brontë and Her Circle.*

Here is possibly another confirming line of development. Since this article was published Miss Muriel West in "The Death of Miles in *The Turn of the Screw*" has argued that the governess exerted much more physical force in extinguishing the life of the child than has been realized by other readers [cf. *PMLA*, LXXIX (June, 1964), 283–88]. Indeed, in the instance from Freud and Breuer, which I cite in my documented version of the essay, the case of "Mrs. Emmy von N.," wherein a boy is frightened to death, some force is applied. And, of course, James was aware of Alice's impulse to do violence to her father. Leon Edel's new and excellent edition of *The Diary* provides further evidence of the extent of Alice's illness.

6   A ROBBER BARON REVISES
THE OCTOPUS

WRITING TO HIS FRIEND Harry Wright on April 5, 1899, of his intention to leave New York for California to gather materials for his next novel, Frank Norris announced that he had "an idea as big as all outdoors." As he wrote, he apparently anticipated no difficulty in fictionalizing the conflict between the Southern Pacific Railroad and the wheat growers in the San Joaquin Valley, his selected subject for *The Octopus*, a name he had already chosen for his novel. As an emergent novelist, charged with imitating the depravity of the French because of *McTeague*, just out in February, Norris felt it would strengthen the public image of himself to choose an American issue of current interest. He proposed to ally himself with H. D. Lloyd, H. H. Boyesen, Edward Bellamy, George D. Herron, Thorstein Veblen, Walter Wyckoff, and others who were assailing the "trusts." Norris rejoiced, moreover, in the encouragement he had for his project from Sam McClure, of Doubleday and McClure Company and founder of *McClure's Magazine*, which was soon to become notorious for its castigation of corruption in high places.

There was, however, a certain rashness in his intent. Prior to coming to New York to read for McClure, Norris had served as assistant editor of the *Wave*, a magazine founded by the publicity man for the Southern Pacific Railroad to promote the Del Monte Hotel, a subsidiary enterprise. Moved to San Francisco before Norris joined it, the *Wave* became the defender of the Southern Pacific against the journalistic attacks of the *Argonaut, Chronicle,* and *Examiner.* In his plan to expose the Railroad, Norris was "shifting sides" and taking on a foe whom he knew to be all-powerful. Yet he could be sanguine about his probable success from the amplitude of treatment given the Railroad's misdeeds in the San Francisco newspapers. Further, he proposed to visit the San Joaquin Valley, where the so-called Mussel Slough affair occurred, to gather further data. If he could substantially document his story, he had little to fear from the Railroad. Besides, the affair had occurred nearly twenty years before, on May 11, 1880. Perhaps no one cared any longer.

The Mussel Slough affair is one of the most tragic in the history of a state whose early chronicles are a kaleidoscope of bloodshed and violence. Through the skillful lobbying of Collis P. Huntington, he and his associates, Leland Stanford, Mark Hopkins, and Charles Crocker, had acquired munificent land grants and financial underwriting by the federal government to enable them to build a railroad to link California to the East by effecting a tie with the Union Pacific, pushing westward. The land grants of 1862 and 1864 gave the promoters, for example, alternate sections, on each side of their tracks, twenty miles in depth in each direction, or 12,800 acres for every mile constructed. Federal and local support, in various forms, are supposed to have lined the pockets of the "Big Four" with a total of seven hundred million dollars on a very small investment (possibly none) by themselves. The story of their success, intricate and devious, is one of the purchase of politicians, commissions, journalists, legislators, judges, congressmen, and even senators to gain their ends. Norris had chosen, not a representative trust, but one of the most efficient machines in the nation to expose.

Some of the California lands acquired by the Railroad, particularly those in Kings, Fresno, and Tulare Counties, were certainly worth no more than the public-lands going price of $2.50 an acre when the Southern Pacific sought settlers for them, for they were arid and sterile. The Railroad distributed circulars inviting settlers to these lands "before patents are issued or the road is completed," declaring its intention "in such cases to sell to them in preference to any other applicant and at a price based upon the value of the land without improvements put upon them by the settlers. . . . The lands are not uniform in price but are offered at various figures from $2.50 upward per acre. . . . Most is for sale at $2.50 to $5.00." Such was the land hunger in Missouri and Illinois that many settlers from those states and elsewhere, thus solicited, moved on to the waste lands which they made fertile by herculean labors, including the digging of a twenty-mile irrigation ditch by volunteer work. To avoid taxes the Railroad had not taken up its patents, but in 1877 it surveyed its line to include the improved lands and requested its patents, though the survey allegedly departed from the route of the promotional materials. Prior to this, the settlers had petitioned Congress to restore the lands to the public since no railroad had been constructed. Characteristically, Congress stalled on this and subsequent petitions. Insecure and alarmed, the ranchers organized a Settlers' League on learning that the patented lands would be thrown on the open market at $25 to $40 an acre and asserted their priority of possession and willingness to pay the government price or $2.50 an acre.

The League instituted a test suit in the Federal Court, and on December 15, 1879, Judge Sawyer ruled against it, allowing an appeal to the Supreme Court. Meanwhile, the Railroad, having sent a land grader or appraiser to the district and his withdrawal having been demanded by the League, responded by bringing uncontested suits of ejectment. Two alien purchasers of contested ranches, Ira Hodge and Perry C. Phillips, were dispossessed by a masked mob; Hodge's house was burned after his furniture was removed, and Phillips' was taken over by a settler. The League purchased rifles and began training a company. Faced with this situation, the Southern Pacific offered land without charge to two men, M. D. Hartt and Walter J. Crow, the latter a known gunman, and called upon A. W. Poole, the U. S. Marshal in the district, to eject the settlers from the properties assigned these "purchasers." Poole, having no choice, went to Hanford, Tulare County, on May 10, 1880, where he was joined by Hartt, Crow, and W. H. Clark, the Railroad's land grader.

On the morning of May 11th, having hired two carriages, the Marshal and Clark drove out of town, followed by the recently "deputized" Hartt and Crow with an arsenal of weapons. Their first stop was at the ranch of W. B. Braden, whom they found away—the Leaguers were holding a picnic—and whose goods they piled in the road. Next they drove to the home of a man named Brewer whom they planned to dispossess. He was at work in an adjacent field, and the Marshal turned his carriage into it, followed at a little distance by Hartt and Crow. At this moment a group of about fifteen settlers appeared, some mounted and some afoot, having been apprised of the invasion. The Marshal, climbing down, was requested not to serve his writs and was presented with a statement of the Leaguers' claims drawn up by Major T. J. McQuiddy, their President; it was pointed out to Poole that their case was still pending in the Supreme Court. When the Marshal replied that he had no alternative, the Leaguers rejoined they would not permit him to serve the writs, asked him to surrender his revolver, and promised him and Clark safe conduct to the nearest station. The Marshal yielded but asked permission to retain his revolver, which was granted.

Hartt and Crow watched with alarm the surrender of the Marshal. "Let's shoot," said Hartt, picking up a rifle.

"Not yet," said Crow, restraining him, "it isn't time."

James Harris, a settler, rode up to their carriage demanding that they give up their arms. For reply, Crow raised a shotgun, loaded with slugs, and deliberately discharged it into Harris' face. Henderson, another settler, drew his revolver and snapped it at Crow, but it did not go off. He shifted his aim to Hartt and shot him in the abdomen as he was descending from the carriage. At almost the same instant he was himself slain by Crow. The latter leaped to the ground firing into the group of settlers. Iver Kneutson was killed before he could draw his revolver; unarmed, Daniel Kelly was shot three times through the body; Archibald McGregor, shot twice through the chest, was hit a third time in the back as he fled. Crow's last victim was Edward Haymaker, struck in the head. With the intervention of J. M. Patterson, a settler, Marshal Poole, and Major McQuiddy, who had just ridden up, firing ceased; Crow took to his heels, disappearing in the wheat, but was trailed, cut off, and slain by an unidentified avenger. Harris, Henderson, and Kneutson had died in the field; Kelly, McGregor, and Hartt were carried into Brewer's house where the first two died before morning. Hartt expired the next day. Only Haymaker of those hit survived the slaughter.

The first news of the affair, unfavorable to the settlers, was given out by the Railroad which closed the nearest telegraph offices against any other version. But the press eventually got the story. So high was feeling in Tulare and Fresno Counties, however, that the only charge lodged against the settlers was that of resisting a U. S. marshal. For this J. J. Doyle, J. M. Patterson (who had stopped the firing), J. D. Purcell, W. L. Pryor, and William Braden were given brief sentences to San Jose prison; an ovation was tendered them on their release. Meanwhile the Supreme Court had ruled for the Southern Pacific, and the settlers, facing eviction, decided to yield to the Railroad, most accepting a rental proposal. The affair at Mussel Slough, starting with a bang, which the court in the resistance case could fix on no one, ended with a whimper.

ii

This was the story Frank Norris found chiefly in the files of the San Francisco *Chronicle* in the Mechanics Library of his native city, for his researches were less extensive than he had meant them to be. Now a celebrity, he was much in demand socially; further, he was engaged to Jeanette Black of that city, to whom he had to dedicate some attention. His chief facts about the lives of the wheat growers were obtained, not from a hurried trip to the town of Tulare, the Bonneville of his novel, but from an extended visit to the San Anita Rancho, near Hollister, owned by Mr. and Mrs. Gaston Ashe. This ranch, part of an original Spanish land grant, which Mrs. Ashe (*née* Dulce Bolado) had inherited, had 5,000 acres of wheat under cultivation. No such extensive plantings then existed in the Tulare region, for the farmers there had been little people and after the conflict with the Railroad had turned to other crops. In California, these little people were known as "sand lappers" from their poverty and the aridity of the area where they settled. Norris altogether neglects their fearful struggle to bring water to the land, and the "irrigating ditch" depicted on the map he drew for his readers is hardly a realistic one and useful only as a refuge rashly abandoned in the fight. Norris "scaled up" the holdings of Magnus Derrick, Annixter, and others to accord with his preconception of an "epic" struggle: *The Octopus* was never intended as a "class" novel—in Norris' eyes the Railroad was the enemy of all Californians, large or small, and his vision called for them to be large. The engineer Dyke and the renter Hooven are the little people of the novel, and even they are not "sand lappers." It was the San Anita Rancho, its life and environs moved 120 miles southeastward, that gave Norris his conception of the ranchers and the setting of their story. Certain traits of Annixter were derived from those of Gaston Ashe, while Mrs. Ashe yielded suggestions for Annie Derrick. A pretty Spanish nurse at the nearby Rita Sande ranch provided Norris with a physical model for Angéle Varian. The flower seed ranch and mission of her background bloomed in Norris' imagination after a number of visits to San Juan Bautista and its old Spanish mission, from the garden of which he could view Morse's Seed Ranch. The town itself became the Guadalajara of *The Octopus*. A dance in the Bolado barn was the basis for Annixter's barn celebration in which he bested the gunman Delaney. Whether Norris worked on the sacking platform of a harvester at the Gates' ranch or near Tulare is uncertain, but the detail of S. Behrman's triumphant experience is that of a participant. That he saw a rabbit roundup near Hanford is conceded.

Norris brought still other things back from California. The story of Dyke is synthesized from that of two train robbers who bore grudges against the Railroad and were regarded as modern Robin Hoods in their region. Chris Evans had been evicted and ruined after the Mussel Slough affair, and John Sontag, a brakeman, held the Railroad responsible for crippling him. After four holdups they eluded arrest with rancher help, but finally they were run down and Sontag was killed. Evans escaped from jail, but after a year of freedom in the Sierras, was tricked into visiting his home on false news of a child's illness, recaptured, and lodged in San Quentin. A gushing dowager, met at an evening party in San Francisco, became the model for Mrs. Cedarquist. Edwin Markham, helpful in the limning of Presley, chose to publish "The Man with the Hoe" in a newspaper, the *Sunday Examiner*, of January 8, 1899, under just the sort of suasion that Presley yields to in the publication of his poem "The Toilers." Norris had the title for his novel, as we have seen, before his trip to California. He remembered from boyhood how the newspaper cartoonists had depicted the Southern Pacific as a giant squid, its tentacles grasping farmer, merchant, legislator, journalist, and shipper; its head, a similacrum of that particular member of the Big Four whom the newspaper wished to castigate.

When Norris returned to New York in October, crammed with material, he was all set to expose his great corporation, his "trust." But things had changed in New York. His publishing house had become Doubleday, Page, and Company, Walter Hinds Page having replaced his sponsor Sam McClure. Furthermore, the company, which had been a little left of center, swung to the right. Norris learned this when he received from Mrs. Tille Lewis Parks, of the editorial department, a nervous letter touching upon his intentions and expressing her own belief in the virtue of corporations. Norris promptly told her that he was "on the other side" and that the Southern Pacific, neither legitimate nor tolerable, was a burning issue in California. After another exchange, Mrs. Parks or someone else in the firm persuaded Norris, or possibly arranged for him, to go see Collis P. Huntington, President of the Southern Pacific, in his New York office, to get the Railroad's version of the conflict.

Then occurred the interview which Norris recorded as Presley's confrontation of Shelgrim, head of the P. & S. W. Railroad. But Norris came away from his interview with more than a sermon on Markham's artistic folly in writing "The Man with the Hoe" and a disquisition on the inevitable working out of the laws of supply and demand. Huntington apparently not only intimidated him, as Presley was intimidated, but lodged a furious charge against the settlers, revealing to Norris for the first time that they, whom he had supposed innocent, had attempted to "pack" the state rate-fixing commission. The railroad magnate did not say how they had aimed at this, for the novelist immediately wrote his politically experienced friend, Isaac Marcosson, confessing that he was in a "beautiful 'political muddle' " and asking how the "ring" of ranchers might have got their man on the commission. Out of new information, whether from Marcosson or elsewhere, Norris manufactured his exciting story of the "equal" culpability of the ranchers, with its reckless but heroic originator Osterman, with its reluctant and finally humiliated Governor, with its treacherous Lyman Derrick, its loyal Harran, and its ever cynical yet faithful Annixter. Norris' visit to the "ogre" of the Southern Pacific changed utterly the emphasis of his novel.

Many factors influenced Norris to seize upon the deeply provoked misbehavior of the ranchers and to develop it fully. The adjustment of his shocked idealism to the reality that Huntington exposed and the strength of Huntington himself, so well-prepared for Norris' advent, had something to do with it. Then he must have realized that this balancing of the scales would be pleasing to his publishers. He hoped to be married soon, but his pen would not support two; possibly he thought to resume his reading for the firm; indeed, he soon did and married Jeanette Black in February, 1900. But was there more to the story? Was he obsessed by his own metaphor and feared if he attacked the Octopus a punishing tentacle would reach for him? Collis P. Huntington had a reputation for neglecting nothing—not even literature. It was he who had put up anonymously $750 for the best answer to Markham's "socialistic" poem, the influence of which he feared in California. How would he have reacted to *The Octopus* as originally planned?

iii

Since the poet Presley is the chief commentator on the story, since he is a detached spectator in the conflict, and since the novel begins and ends with his observations, it is a natural assumption that he speaks for the novelist. Yet he should be only partially identified with Norris, for in the preliminary sketch Norris made for Presley, there are traits he would hardly have assigned to himself—irrationality, for example. That Presley is swayed by the anarchist dynamiter, Caraher, to avenge his friends by throwing a futile bomb into the home of the Railroad's agent, S. Behrman, and then regretting it, as well as his intemperate "Red" speech at the memorial service, are evidence enough that Norris stuck to his preconception. The poet, though impulsive, seems an educable, sensitive spirit, exposed to violent conflict and partisan through friendship and sensitivity, whose "education" forms a major strand in the story. Norris made him the author of a poem called "The Toilers," very like "The Man with the Hoe," possibly in deliberate defiance of Huntington, while allowing the magnate of the novel to overwhelm him. An open, unprepared mind is never the equal of a ready, closed one, and to think of Presley confounding Shelgrim is to indulge in absurdity. Huntington made Norris reconsider his story while Shelgrim only temporarily astounds Presley. Shelgrim's presence, dress, and details of his office are so exactly those of Huntington's appearance and mode of work that the stunning effect of trying to

challenge him is probably the purest verisimilitude. But
Presley recovers; dining with the wealthy Gerards while
Mrs. Hooven is starving, Presley reflects on Shelgrim's
specious defense: "The Railroad might indeed be a force
only, which no man could control and for which no man
was responsible, but his friends had been killed and years
of extortion and oppression had wrung money from all the
San Joaquin, money which had made possible this very
scene in which he found himself. Because Magnus had
been beggared, Gerard had become Railroad King; because
the farmers of the valley were poor, these men were rich."
He adds his own conviction that "the People *would* turn
some day, and turning, rend those who now preyed upon
them."

But Presley's thought is not the author's until it is
qualified by the experience of the "shepherd-prophet"
Vanamee. Visiting for the last time the site of the epic
struggle, Presley views the sleeping valley, its wheat all
harvested, from the range above and comes to the conclusion that men are nothing, "mere ephemerides," and that
"FORCE" is everything. Shortly after this, however, he
joins his friend Vanamee whom he has seen below. The
shepherd has had both a devastating and restorative
experience. The lovely Angéle whom he adored had been
raped and had died in childbirth. Returning ever to the
spot of their trysts and her ravishment, Vanamee, unable
to avenge himself upon the never-revealed rapist, by
concentration of the will has called Angéle back—or
rather, her perfect semblance in her daughter who becomes his bride. Out of his personal experience of grief and
restitution Vanamee counsels Presley, and Presley accepts
his counsel: "You are all broken, all cast down by what you
have seen in this valley, this hopeless struggle, this
apparently hopeless despair. . . . What remains? . . .
Try to find that . . . and you will find, if your view be
large enough, that it is *not* evil, but good, that in the end
remains."

Norris' faith, expressed through a mystic who has an
unusual, not to say extraordinary experience, is not sup-

ported by the main action of the novel, unless we count the poetic justice visited upon S. Behrman as an adequate resolution for the tragedy. However despicable, S. Behrman is not the Railroad and none of its magnates is reached by the events. They were too far above the battle. S. Behrman is the best surrogate Norris could devise and Behrman's destruction by the wheat itself as a force is highly deserved. But the Greeks never visited the wrath of the gods solely on surrogates. Nor can we quite accept the punishment of Behrman as an earnest of further justice to come. The railroad magnates will be bypassed, as indeed in life they were.

In his essay, "The Novel with a 'Purpose,'" Norris declares this to be the highest form of fiction, cites *Les Misérables* as an illustration, and cautions the creator of such a novel against letting his purpose run away with him as Zola had permitted it to do in *Fécondité*. In a peculiar sense Norris' admonition is wholly a self-admonition. Naïvely thinking the ranchers guiltless, he had discovered them to be speculators and corrupt. In the carefully developed story of Magnus Derrick he works out a punishment in excess of the crime, with an inevitability that is thoroughly satisfying. But the more enormous crime of the Railroad owners, while adequately indicted, remains only punished symbolically through S. Behrman's fate. Was this a matter of self-restraint? We know that *The Octopus*, followed by *The Pit*, in each of which evil comes comfortably off, were parts of a trilogy to be climaxed by *The Wolf* in which American wheat was to relieve a famine in Europe. Even in *The Octopus* the very wheat that smothers the consciousness of S. Behrman is intended to relieve the famished in India and is provided by the largesse of the mulcts of the ranchers. In "the larger view," recommended by Vanamee, the wheat is a divine force predestined to accomplish good. The theme, reinforced by Norris' careful avoidance of revenge, suggests the romantic assurance of Victor Hugo. But was Norris satisfied with this, or did he mean to contrive an adequate *fictional* punishment for the greater malefactors in *The*

Wolf? There can be no final answer, but Norris' realism, responsible for his better writing, would very likely have inhibited him.

Most of Norris' difficulties arose from the fact that he was an American and a Californian, therefore essentially optimistic, a believer in progress under the mild supervision of God. As an artist, however, he had been fascinated by the methods of the French naturalists, particularly those of Zola. Disillusioned by the successive failures of French republicanism and contemptuous of their middle class, the French naturalists were pessimistic determinists, interested in depicting the degeneracy of man. Where no deeply felt issues involving his countrymen were concerned, Norris could perfectly imitate them, as he had done in *McTeague*. Had he been content with a French conclusion he would have produced the American equivalent of *La Terre* or *Fécondité*, and easily a better book than either, for he readily achieves a sense of the fecund earth and the fecund woman, borrowed from these books, and his characterizations are infinitely better than Zola's. Magnus Derrick, Harran, Hooven, and Annixter live. But he would have been false to himself and his America. After all, Californians conceded, the Big Four *did* complete the railroad and confer a prodigious future on California. They could not have done it without boodling and plundering, for no one and no combination of persons in California was wealthy enough to do it. Norris stopped short of conceding them divine appointment to do so, even though it would have been consistent with his ideas of creating an American epic, for, occupying the position of the Greek gods, Huntington and his pals were immune, like the gods, to punishment. Melville, *déraciné* and bitter, achieved immortality in the only way open to Norris, who believed that "force" is a manifestation of "primordial energy flung out from the hand of the Lord God himself, immortal, calm, infinitely strong"—by quarreling with Deity. In this way solely could he have fused his book with the right Promethean fire. But what was consistent and plausible with *Moby Dick* in 1851, at the height of the Romantic

movement, might have been consistent, yet utterly im-
plausible with *The Octopus* in 1901. The invulnerable
monsters of these representative books belong to quite
different orders of reality.

AFTERWORD

Like my essay on Howells, this is a study of the
pressures that may be exerted on a writer of genius to force
him to alter his work. Anyone who reads *The Octopus* is
aware of Norris' confused intent and has an impulse to
inquire into its causes, for his courage had been demonstrated in writing *McTeague*, a palpable contribution to
Zolaesque literature when that literature was hardly respectable in America. Long ago convinced of the power of
economics in human thinking, I started looking for the
forces exerted on Norris. Was the Mussel Slough affair a
dead issue? Apparently not—at least to one of the great
"robber barons" of the nineteenth century. A personal
pressure was possibly applied to Norris such as, to my
knowledge, was never exerted on Henry James. Then I had
to go into the personal situation of Norris at the time to
find why he yielded. This is my story, but obviously I
cannot write Q.E.D. after it. To do that, unless other
evidence is found, I should have had to have a non-
existent tape-recorder concealed in some one's office, and I
am not sure I am up to that, even in the defense of
literature. I venture that the episode took the heart out of
Norris and that this explains the flatulence of *The Pit*.

H. L. MENCKEN OF BALTIMORE. Before his critics tired of defining him, Mencken found himself described as a deflated Nietzsche and an inflated George Ade, a gabby philosopher and a pontifical journalist, a piperaceous philologist and Anheuser's own brightest boy. He was also called a pestilential nuisance, a common scold, a rantipole, an intellectual Houyhnhnm, a literary Uhland, and other things by those less interested in definition. It was a lively game, finding epithets to hurl at this Baltimore Oriole, who was himself the best pitcher of epithets in any league, with an assortment of fast ones, spitters, and knucklers. In fact, his own word-horde, in the parlance of the Anglo-Saxons, was the best arsenal for his contemners. But neither Mencken nor his critics ever thought of him as a plumed knight, a lofty cavalier, a zealot, and a crusader. This role, though overlaid and heavily camouflaged, was as natural to him as any, and if he is viewed in it, he stands clear as a rather simple but strongly motivated person. Better take him, however, on a major crusade, like his effort to awaken the South, rather than on a short foray, like his trip to Boston to sell the *Mercury*, banned in that home of light, on "Brimstone Corner" of the Common.

Back in the twenties, when Mencken's "Americanism" was to English critics his most salient trait, Ernest Boyd observed that Mencken's "patriotism" took "the extreme form of parochialism"—Maryland, or even Baltimore, provided all his standards of judgment. With his preference for German friends, beer, and music, Mencken does not seem a typical Marylander, yet the fact is, he is attached to his native state in every conceivable way. Beer and music give the German contingent in Maryland a complacency about their lot there which cannot be distinguished from the relaxed airs of the Calvert collateral. Mencken has never been able to conceive a better existence than his city provides. A third generation Baltimorean, he made life needlessly burdensome to himself when he was editing the *Mercury*, by commuting to New York rather than taking up quarters in the metropolis. Excluding the Eastern Shore, he is purely panegyric when he writes on Maryland for outlanders:

> . . . Freed, by the providence of God, from drought and dervishes, the cyclones and circular insanities of the Middle West, and from the moldering doctrinairism and appalling bugaboos of the South, and from the biological decay of New England, and from the incurable corruption and menacing unrest of the other industrial states, it (Maryland) represents the ideal toward which the rest of the Republic is striving. It is safe, fat, and unconcerned. It can feed itself and have plenty to spare. . . . It has its own national hymn and a flag older than the Stars and Stripes. It is the home of the oyster, of the deviled crab, of hog and hominy, of fried chicken *a la Maryland*. . . . I depict, you may say, Utopia, Elysium, the New Jerusalem. . . .

Traditionally a Baltimorean looks southwards indulgently, and Mencken's biographers, Goldberg, Kemler, and Manchester, make it clear that Henry Louis Mencken had his full share of this indulgence. His grandfather, Burchard Ludwig Mencken, was a Confederate sympathizer and might have joined Lee's army had not lameness made him a liability rather than an asset as a soldier. Mencken's own references to the Civil War have a mixed character: "The South was plainly more gallant, but even the gallantry of the South was largely illusory." Yet on one point he is firmly consistent: the South, prior to the War, had come nearer to achieving the good life than any other part of the country, but it destroyed and dispersed the aristocracy, after which the poor whites had taken over and conferred their mediocrity upon the whole region. Like many a Southerner (compare him with Faulkner), he holds the Negro superior to the poor white. Satisfied with an ethnological explanation for the backwardness of the South and sentimentally disposed towards the region, Mencken spared belaboring it until 1917. To be sure, there were many jocular references to the retarded culture of the South and the witlessness of its peoples in the stuff that Mencken wrote for *Smart Set* and the *Sunpapers*, but these references had more of the character of badinage than of astringent criticism. They had less edge, in fact, than his customary teasing of the "Baltimoralists."

But in November, 1917, in the New York *Evening Mail*, Mencken unleashed what is by all odds the most unrestrained diatribe ever directed against the South—"The Sahara of the Bozart." His deadly seriousness in the attack may be gauged from the fact that he expanded it in *Smart Set* and again in *Prejudices: Second Series* (1920). He trotted out his usual ethnological explanation for the cultural "vacuity" of the region, but he garnished it now with the most intemperate observations, for example, "some of the worst blood of western Europe flows in the veins of the poor whites, now poor no longer." They are largely descendant of the bastards of indentured female servants, who were, according to Bruce, the off-scourings of Europe. Their blood has never been improved, for they were so degraded that the masters of the master-class avoided illicit relations with them, choosing their mistresses among the cleanlier Negresses. Thus the quality of the mulatto has risen; even genius has budded from this grafted stem: "No Southern composer has ever written music so good as that of half a dozen white-black composers who might be named." Even in politics, despite the attention the Southerner has given to the leading question—the race issue, the Negro has excelled him: he has written the only books on the issue that have interested the rest of the world. Comparisons are said to be odious, but this particular sort of comparison was the most offensive that could be designed—and Mencken knew it.

But the main charge is "sterility"—the South is artistically, intellectually, and culturally as sterile as the Sahara Desert. One looks there in vain for a dry-point etcher, a sociologist, an historian, a poet, a philosopher, or even an oboe player of any real distinction. In the entire South there are not as many first-rate men as can be found on a single acre in Europe. "If the whole of the late Confederacy were to be engulfed by a tidal wave tomorrow, the effect upon the civilized minority of men in the world would be but little greater than that of a flood on the Yang-Tse-Kiang." Virginia is the best state in the South, yet no Northern state compares with it in degradation. Her *per capita* expenditures upon her common schools is less than half of that of any Northern state; her colleges are little better than "Baptist seminaries"—not a single contribution to human knowledge has come out of them in a quarter of a century. Her political figures are job-seekers and time-servers. A Washington or a Jefferson, restored to Virginia by a caprice of fate, would be excoriated as a scoundrel and clapped in jail. Chivalry is utterly dead. Virginia can, however, claim the only prose-writer in the South, James Branch Cabell, whose presence only emphasizes the bleakness of the area. But if the situation in the Old Dominion is bad, that in Georgia is worse—and Georgia makes the loudest claims to "progress." "There the liberated lower orders of whites have borrowed the worst commercial bounderism of the Yankee and superimposed it on a culture that, at bottom, is little removed from savagery. Georgia is at once the home of the cotton-mill sweater and of the most noisy and vapid sort of chamber of commerce, of the Methodist parson turned Savonarola, and of the lynching bee. A self-respecting European going there to live, would not only find intellectual stimulation utterly lacking; he would actually feel a certain insecurity, as if the scene were the Balkans or the China Coast." There is more, much more, and some of it worse, but this is a sampling.

It is interesting to speculate why Mencken turned suddenly and with such violence upon the South. The reference to Cabell may be a clue, but it is no clear thumbprint on a broken pane of window glass; one should not infer that this was an elaborate way of bringing a recently discovered novelist to the attention of his section, though that as a partial motive, need not be dismissed. Generosity with *bravura* is more characteristic of Mencken than is supposed. Cabell's *The Cream of the Jest* had just been discovered by Southern-born Burton Rascoe whose enthusiastic review brought it to Mencken's attention. The latter was ever after a stanch supporter of Cabell and wrote an introduction to one of his books. A better surmise than that "The Sahara of the Bozarts" was written just to promote Cabell, however, is that Mencken took the emergence of Cabell and Rascoe, together with that of two minor poets whom he also mentions, as proof that the South was about to rise from the lethargy of sixty years and contribute something to the cultural life of the nation. Timely and vigorous use of the goad might help. There are hints in the essay of the exasperated lover that the flood of derision does not quite obscure. Take the last lines, for example. "The Southerner, at his worst," Mencken tells us, "is never quite the surly cad that the Yankee is. . . . In the main he is a pleasant fellow—hospitable, polite, good-humored, even jovial. . . . But a bit absurd . . . a bit pathetic. . . ."

In composing his attack Mencken indubitably had in his mind the furious castigation of the South that Mark Twain had undertaken in *Life on the Mississippi* and had completed in *The Adventures of Hucklebury Finn*. Twain had execrated the vulgarity of taste in the Southern home, in books, in music. Twain had ridiculed grotesque expressions of a chivalric impulse in female education and public architecture in the South. Twain had belabored the South for feuding and duelling, for lynching parties, and general ignorance. A more benighted yokelry than that which appeared to witness the King and the Duke perform in "The Royal Nonesuch" possibly was never represented in fiction. Mencken, an inveterate admirer of Twain, saw, as everyone else has seen, that affection inspired Twain's assault and found in it the license for his own corrective.

The major effort of Mencken's critical career might have been made as a scourge to the South had not fate intervened in the person of Stuart P. Sherman. In September, 1917, Mencken published A *Book of Prefaces*, his most serious critical effort up to that time and one of the books by which he will be ultimately judged. Besides long studies of Joseph Conrad, Huneker, and Dreiser, it contains the famous essay "Puritanism as a Literary Force." Though the essay ranges from Victorian prudery to insolent Comstockery, with scintillating raillery at the idiocies that censorship can produce, the most original point made is that Puritanism is not exclusive New England "madness"; it is in the South that it "takes on its most bellicose and extravagant forms." The point is buttressed with an ethnological argument, touching the distribution of the "kirk-crazy Scotch and that plupious and beauty-hating folk, the Scotch-Irish," that has considerable force. This is an obvious further development of the attack begun in "The Sahara of the Bozarts." But Stuart P. Sherman was asked to review A *Book of Prefaces* for *The Nation*; he had not discerned what Mencken was trying to do, and at that time he probably would not have been interested had he discerned. Sherman was merely incensed at Mencken's irreverence and his want of standards; Sherman's review was ironically called "Beautifying American Letters"; it hardly touched the content of Mencken's book but assailed him as a German (remember we were at war with Germany) in an apparent effort to silence him. Rascoe and other *avant-garde* critics rallied to Mencken and war was on—a war that proved to be a protracted one, with "Puritanism" as its central issue, that absorbed Mencken's chief energies and in which he was the ultimate victor. To indulge in pure speculation, had Mencken been allowed to pursue his Southern crusade uninterrupted, he would have soon consolidated the emerging Southern writers, who would have recognized his intent, and then he might have turned upon New York, which in 1917, needed ventilating as much as any place on earth. As titular head of the Southern renascence he might have acquired the urbanity which is his chief deficiency as a critic.

Because of his war with Sherman, Mencken conducted his Southern crusade for a time with his left hand, so to speak, but it was an artful and insistent left hand. In the course of his writing, he frequently managed to tuck in something calculated to stir resentment south of the Potomac, or more exactly, to shape effort there. He could do the Southern congressman as no one has ever done him; he was full of ironic suggestions for the conduct of life: "The Ku Klux Klan, it seems to me, is a good influence in the South rather than a bad one, for it tends to regulate and formalize the normal sport of the people, and so restrains excess. . . ." He shifted the focus of his attention from Georgia to Arkansas as culturally the most dismal spot on earth, agreeing in this with his mentor, Mark Twain. "I know New Yorkers who have been in Cochin China, Kafiristan, Paraguay, Somaliland, and West Virginia, but not one who has ever penetrated the miasmatic jungles of Arkansas." Edgar Kimler has told the amusing story of how the president of the Arkansas Advancement Association tried to get Mencken deported as an alien but failed when it was discovered that he was a native son.

The climax of Mencken's Southern crusade came in the Scopes trial in Dayton, Tennessee, in 1925. Possibly inspired by Mencken who had been blasting away at anti-evolution laws which forbade the teaching of Darwinism in the schools of certain Southern states, John Thomas Scopes, of Dayton, deliberately defied the law in his state and was arrested and brought to trial. Sensing the journalistic possibilities of the event, the owner of the *Sunpapers* not only provided Scopes with bail before his trial, but sent two of his best reporters, a cartoonist, and H. L. Mencken to cover the trial. The latter turned it into a journalistic carnival. The participation of Clarence Darrow in the defense and of William Jennings Bryan in the prosecution is so well known as to need no recital. But in Dayton the person who was most resented was Mencken, for his stories in the Baltimore papers were widely syndicated, especially in the South. Only the cool reasoning of the local bank president, A. P. Haggard, kept a crowd one night from riding Mencken out of town on a rail. He left before the jury decided that Scopes was guilty, but from the security of Baltimore wrote the most dreadful mock-eulogy of William Jennings Bryan, who, exhausted by his efforts and the fearful heat, collapsed and died five days after Scopes' conviction. American journalism respects no proprieties, but here perhaps Mencken went too far. There was talk about boycotting Baltimore products if that city's leading journalist and critic were not restrained. Nothing ever came of it, however, for there was recognition everywhere that, indictable as he might be for bad taste, Mencken was profoundly right. The Bryans represented regression. The anti-evolution laws might remain on the books but they would hardly be enforced, even in the aridest and sandiest parts of the Sahara.

Like Aaron's rod, Mencken's goad had proved itself a symbol of fertility. By 1925 the Southern renascence was well under way. It began in 1921, with the first issue of *The Reviewer*, founded in Richmond by Emily Clark and her friends, appearing on the bookstands in February and containing, among other things, an appreciative review of Mencken's *Prejudices: Second Series*, which contained "The Sahara of the Bozarts" in its final form. Miss Clark has given so witty an account of this periodical and of the persons connected with it in her *Innocense Abroad* that a rehearsal here would be a dull travesty, but it is permissible, surely, to name some of the distinguished contributors. Besides Mencken, one notes in the tables of contents Achmed Abdullah, Hervey Allen, Henry Bellaman, Edwin Bjorkman, Ernest Boyd, James Branch Cabell, Barrett Clark, Babette Deutsch, Paul Eldridge, Ronald Firbank, John Galsworthy, Ellen Glasgow, Douglas Goldring, Paul Green, Sara Haardt, Joseph Hergesheimer, Du Bose Heyward, Addison Hibbard, Robert Hillyer, Guy Holt, Gerald W. Johnson, Mary Johnston, Margery Lattimer, Amy Lowell, Arthur Machen, Edwin Muir, Robert Nathan, Frances Newman, James Oppenheimer, Julia Peterkin, Burton Rascoe, Ben Ray Redman, Agnes Repplier, Lynn Riggs, Vincent Starrett, Gertrude Stein, George Sterling, Allen Tate, Louis Untermeyer, Carl Van Vechten, and

Elinor Wylie—a cosmopolitan list, including the names of many contributors whom Mencken interested in *The Reviewer*, but also a very high percentage of new Southern writers. "To appear in *The Reviewer*," James Branch Cabell has written, "became, throughout the insecure small world of American letters, a species of accolade." And Southern writers, making their debut there, were by that fact recommended to the more substantial, but less courageous magazines of the North. It was natural that some of them passed effortlessly, it would seem, from *The Reviewer* to Mr. Mencken's *Mercury*, founded at the end of 1923.

It cannot be claimed, of course, that Mencken was the chief instigator of the Southern renascence. Others made notable contributions. One recalls with gratitude what Ferdinand Koch did for playwriting and even for the novel while he taught at the University of North Carolina, how Freeman and Hubbell have strengthened historical scholarship, what Howard Odum and Roark Bradford have done to preserve folklore, and best of all, the inspiration furnished a score of writers by Sherwood Anderson's one year of residence in New Orleans. But to lengthen this list does not diminish Mencken's importance. If not the prime instigator, he was at least one of the chief movers. His influence was more pervasive than can ever be gauged. Richard Wright has told how he first learned of Mencken through an editorial in the Memphis *Commercial Appeal* which ended with one hot, short sentence, "Mencken is a fool!" Timorously he bought a *Mercury* and shortly his ambition for his career was formed. And Wright's report could be duplicated many times. The "Sage of Baltimore" was a better sectionalist than has been admitted.

If Mencken were not incapacitated today, how would he view the South? Thirty-five years have passed since "The Sahara of the Bozarts" first appeared in the New York *Evening Mail*. In William Faulkner the South can claim a major novelist and Nobel Prize winner; even Georgia and Arkansas can boast distinguished poets in Conrad Aiken and John Gould Fletcher. A Texan has just written the longest American novel. Thomas Hart Benton, of the new American school—new no longer—is most likely to survive. It would seem that Mencken would have to admit, not from these distinguished examples alone but from a multiplicity of evidence, that the "desert" had started burgeoning. But would he? Never—if he acted in character. The goad would be wickedly applied again in the hope of still finer results. And who shall assert it might not bring them? What has Mobile to boast of, save a good restaurant? Is there a bookstore there? Or does anyone own a violoncello?

AFTERWORD

No one enjoyed H. L. Mencken more than I did in the twenties: his masterly use of hyperbole, his iconoclasm, his gusto were very captivating. At the same time I had an itchy annoyance with his persistent attacks on pedagogues (of whom I was one) whom he bested in every encounter. More or less for sport, and certainly to tease, I derided him in *Intellectual America* employing a feeble but recognizable imitation of his own exuberant style to do so. Granville Hicks, under whose appreciative eye my manuscript then fell, told me, as I remember, that I should work harder at my burlesque or abandon it. I let it stand. Though written in the thirties, due to much revising elsewhere, my book was not published until later when Mencken's prestige had sadly waned and I am told that he was hurt by it. "Mencken and the South," written for the *Georgia Review*, was a deliberately propitiatory act to his troubled and troublesome spirit. It celebrates a much neglected aspect of his contribution to American literature.

THE PRETERNATURAL ABSORPTION of the modern reader in the disfigured and unfigurable souls of fictive monsters provides one of the puzzles of our times. Physical monstrosity is revolting to us, so revolting that we expect the literary man to match the silence of the embryologist on the subject. And despite his penchant for the horrific and his irritation at restraint in all other matters, the modern writer has accepted the taboo. After all, the cretins of Faulkner and Steinbeck are not much more offensive than Quasimodo and Caliban, who have a quality of poetry about them. Yet the modern reader not merely tolerates but is fascinated by psychical anomalies, by grotesques, by distortions of all that is symmetrical in our supposed conception of man's spirit. Do we lack the power to visualize the shape of the souls of men that we accept in fiction warped natures whose accretions and deficiencies outmode any malformations of embryonic reproduction? Or is the fault the writer's? Has his want of perception robbed his caricature of the human spirit of all purport? Why is our imagination less affected by the psychical monstrosity than by the physical?

No writer in our time has been more possessed by the literary potentialities of the monster than has Robert Penn Warren; hence we may as properly survey his work as that of another for answers to our queries. With Warren, moreover, we can quickly satisfy ourselves on one score. It is a psychological or artistic compulsion which has induced him to study distorted characters and not a calculated desire to achieve fame through sensationalism. Relatively obscure until the Pulitzer prize came to him, he has persistently abjured notoriety for the sake of his art. A Kentuckian by birth and a Rhodes scholar after study at Vanderbilt, the University of California, and Yale, Robert Penn Warren had taught in five colleges and had had his name inscribed on double that number of books before the Pulitzer committee chose to honor *All the King's Men*. With Cleanth Brooks, Jr., he had brought the teaching and critical methods of F. R. Leavis to America. It is commonly said that *Understanding Poetry* "revolution-ized" the teaching of that subject in our colleges; it appears, however, to one observer still to be taught more or less as it always was—with fitful success by the best teachers. But Warren had also been a member of the Fugitive group of poets at Vanderbilt (he is easily the most obscure and difficult of that group) and one of the promoters of the *Southern Review*. He has been occupied with other things than his own aggrandizement. It cannot possibly be inferred that his persistent delineation of the monster is a bold throw for public attention.

There is no hint of the author's motivation in his prefaceless first book, *John Brown: The Making of a Martyr* (1929). The victim of the official hangman's knot of December 2, 1859, cannot be conceived to have been haunting southern bedsteads, even in the back country, when Mr. Warren turned to him. Brown is scarcely treated as a Negrophile but rather as a person fanatically sure of "his own worth." In a final summary of the captain's character his biographer notes: "Superb energy, honesty and fraud, chicanery, charity, thrift, endurance, cruelty, conviction, murder, and prayer—they all had failed, only to leave him surer than before that he was right and that his plans were 'right in themselves.'" Mr. Warren, how-ever, does not skewer all his events on this theme. "Murder for profit," for example, is his motivation for the Kansas career of his protagonist: the victims of the Potawatomi massacre were fat victims, and their horses and other movable property instigated their butchery. Without disputing this, one realizes that it could not have been a complete cause: Old Brown took exactly as many lives as had been taken by the proslavery raid on Lawrence. The revenge motive certainly operated, and to admit its operation is to concede more than megalomania as a driving force for the fanatic.

Warren's tendency to explain each revealing episode by whatever is least creditable to Brown turns the old man into an authentic monster, more giant squid than human and more amorphous than defined. But we are not filled with loathing because there is a patent disparity between what this unjelled protoplasm could have accomplished and the actual achievement of the successful revolutionary. A wounded captive, beyond any reprieve, John Brown understood that he could still set in motion a chain of events culminating in cataclysm. "Christ, the great capitain, . . . saw fit to take from me the sword of steel after I had carried it for a time; but he put another in my hand, ['the sword of the Spirit']." Only a man possessed could have played for Brown's result, and Warren misses the true exaltation of that possession. He might have made the zealot out a villain, but the monster he could not. Thus the reader who remains unmoved by Warren's John Brown can charge his apathy up to the author. However misshapen and sinister Brown was, he had more purport than Warren ever allows him.

Possibly puzzled at his failure, the author turned to the zealot again in *Night Rider* (1939). Percy Munn is not a fanatic when we first meet him: he is a somewhat rigid, scrupulous young man who raises tobacco and practices law in a fashion to gain him local esteem. But he becomes fanatical by the degrees of his involvement, first, in the Association of Growers of Dark Fired Tobacco and, second, in the Brotherhood for the Protection and Control, which is the "pressure organization" to influence recalcitrant growers to join up. The purpose of the association is to secure higher prices from the buyers by joint withholding. The events of the novel parallel those of the "Tobacco War" of 1905–8 in the burley and dark tobacco regions of Kentucky when the farmers, incensed at the low prices offered them by the buyers of the newly organized Tobacco Trust, turned and bit the hand that had been niggardly feeding them, blowing up and firing warehouses, derailing trains and the like, until Governor Willson called out the militia and restored order. Though Warren describes the organized night attack on the warehouses at "Bardsville," in which his hero participated, his chief emphasis is on the measures of intimidation resorted to by the night riders of the protective Brotherhood—"no blackguards and riff-raff, only worthy and respectable men with a good name in their community"— who "scrape" the young plants of farmers allergic to the association, burn or dynamite their curing barns, set fire to their homes, horsewhip the owners, drive them out of the region, and murder intransigents and traitors to the cause. All these activities, however, better reveal the fanatic than would such a conflict as Frank Norris describes in *The Octopus* and somewhat justify Mr. Warren in making no reference whatsoever to the Tobacco Trust.

Warren does an extraordinarily subtle and ingenious thing in turning the reasonable Mr. Munn into a zealot. So cunningly is the change managed that it is a well-established fact before the reader is aware that it has taken place. When Percy Munn's wife leaves him, our sympathies are adroitly kept with the husband; we forget that May had begged him to "Love me, Perse. Love me always." We ignore the fact that his nights abroad are unexplained to the wife who must put a different connotation on them than the reader does, though here—and with what artfulness—Warren allows his protagonist to sleep with another woman. We even forget that when wife and husband drift apart Mr. Munn acknowledges that the fault is his. "But she had not changed. She was as she had always been. Whatever change there was—and there was a change, she was right when she accused him—was in him. He knew that." We spare Perse Munn because already our sympathies are enlisted on his side in the struggle to make the association work; we spare him more especially because Warren very ingeniously sends May to live with an aunt whose rebuff of the formally repentant husband springs from a nature so abnormal that we wonder what the wife could be to turn to it for comfort. It is only in retrospect, when we revert to Munn's murder at a quarry's edge of a man whom he had once saved from the gallows that we exclaim that he who did this thing is mad or close to being mad. Even here there are extenuating circumstances, for not only had the victim attempted blackmail against a member of the association but he had let Mr. Munn, in that earlier event, send an innocent man to his death. It is only later that we see that all the extenuating things are the author's dodges to adumbrate Mr. Munn's drift toward that kind of mania which possesses the fanatic. Even the resignation of Captain Todd, whom Munn had hitherto respected, does not teach us that the hero is now in the lunatic fringe of the movement. Never was character change more adroitly managed in a novel.

But the story goes all to pieces. A necessary witness to the prosecution of one of the ringleaders of the night riders is assassinated by a sharpshooter firing from Mr. Munn's office window, and he, who had taken flight for another reason, is the assumed murderer. From this point on, Robert Penn Warren flounders, apparently at a loss to know how to make an end to his narrative. Stalling for inspiration, he has Mr. Munn take refuge with one Willie Proudfit who delays the denouement by spinning out his own story, one so alien to *Night Rider* that it cannot be regarded as an excrescence but rather as a dead weight "chunked down" on the living substance of the tale. Indeed, Warren had previously published it as a short story ("How Willie Proudfit Came Home") in the *Southern Review*, and his resort to it here plainly signifies desperation—a temporary inability to invent further in Mr. Munn's story. But, wrenching himself past this block, he does invent a culmination to the tale. Lucille Christian, who had been Percy Munn's mistress until paralysis struck down her father—his shock coming from the discovery that his friend had used his home to dally with his daughter—finds the fugitive at the Proudfits' and suggests flight to the West with him, only to be stonily refused. Then Munn seeks out ruined Senator Tolliver to kill him, either because of Tolliver's share as a turncoat in defeating the night riders or, as the boys would say, because he had made "passes" at Lucille. But Munn lacks the nerve to kill Tolliver in sickbed—even as "a favor." Surrounded at Tolliver's home by militiamen who have been tipped off as to his presence, Mr. Munn dies in a blaze of gunfire in an open field—an ambiguous monster. Only inhumanity can explain his rejection of Lucille and his election to die in Kentucky where his cause is a lost cause. His choice, furthermore, convicts him of the assassination with which he was falsely charged. But martyrdom, even of this unnecessary sort, cloaks his monstrosity to a degree and leaves the reader confused. It is plain from the outset that Warren does not wish to move us to compassion for Mr. Munn—he keeps him aloof by the constant use of "Mr." (Munn even thinks of himself as "Mr. Munn"). Yet his cause is presented to elicit reader sympathy. Elevated by this, with his zealotry glossed cunningly by the author, Mr. Munn becomes vague and indecipherable. Warren needs to unswathe him at the end of the tale. The space allotted to Willie Proudfit should be devoted to a clarification of Munn's attitudes toward Tolliver and Lucille; his own fixation needs analysis. We do not see him finally as a clearly defined monster. *Night Rider* is a grand failure, but it is a failure nevertheless.

Perhaps a better way than direct portraiture to reveal the malignantly deformed character is to show the effect of the character on other people. At least, that is the method Robert Penn Warren has resorted to in his last two novels, *At Heaven's Gate* (1943) and *All the King's Men* (1946). In the former badly titled book the monster is Bogan Murdock, financier, manipulator, and boss of a southern state which bears some resemblance to Tennessee. Like Crump, Bogan Murdock is head of a bond- and share-house; and, like the titular master of Tennessee, Murdock can be suave and charming. But he can also be deadly. It is his power to contaminate many people that fascinates Warren; and, for effectiveness, the novelist goes too far in tracing Murdock's influence. "The trouble with the novel as a whole," Malcolm Cowley has observed, "is that it tells too many stories in too many styles." But one story, that of Sue Murdock, Bogan's lovely daughter, is central, and the author's success or failure must be judged from it. Sue is no different from countless other girls of her age; she has a rich, warm nature, a curiosity about the world and her own emotions, and a resolute desire to be herself. Very naturally, she has tried intercourse before she throws herself at Jerry Calhoun, an "All-American" back whom her father has acquired to sell bonds. But as Jerry becomes more and more the man Bogan desires (Bogan makes him vice-president, in charge of securities, in the Southern Fidelity Bank which he founds), he becomes less and less to Sue's taste; finally, she ends their engagement and leaves her own home to live with a bohemian crowd which fluctuates around Slim Sarrett, poet and prize fighter, whose mistress she elects to be. Jerry, sent by Bogan to her address, is rebuffed; so is her brother and finally Bogan himself. Meanwhile it is brutally revealed to Sue that Slim is a sexual pervert, and, shuddering away from him, she gives herself to Jason Sweetwater, a labor leader with convictions against marriage, who gets her pregnant. Neglected by Sweetwater during a strike, she takes to drink, threatens to have an abortion if he will not marry her, excites Sarrett into a collision with Sweetwater in which he is bested, and finally yields, not to the last entreaty of her father, but to death, whose emissary is the poet and prize fighter (the "lark" at heaven's gate?).

Jerry Calhoun is properly drawn, and so, too, despite the trouble some reviewers had in realizing it, is Sue Murdock. They are complementary to each other in showing the effect of the dominance of Bogan Murdock: Jerry becomes entranced, incapable of deserting Murdock when the latter takes from him his father's home, supine even when he is forewarned that he will be made a cat's-paw in the failure of Southern Fidelity. Sue becomes, on the other hand, hysterically resistant—her sexual indulgence is not libertinism but a form of mad rebellion. That she should make a final play for the depraved poet rather than return to her father is a choice that reveals how hideous in her sight is Bogan Murdock, despite his profession of affection—a profession exposed by the gratitude with which he accepts her sensational murder, filling the papers when his affairs are under investigation and saving his scalp. But Slim Sarrett and Jason Sweetwater, who are themselves freakish monsters, contribute not at all to the limning of Bogan. Could Warren have drawn these aberrant creatures into the orbit of his major rascal and made their evil an infusion of his poison, he would better have pointed up his tale.

Some of the best writing in *At Heaven's Gate* has nothing to do with the father-daughter relationship. Interspersed throughout the narrative are sections from a long defensive epistle written by Ashby Wyndham, street evangelist, who is awaiting trial for inciting his followers to fire upon the police. In effect, this is the Willie Proudfit material integrated in the novel; and because Robert Penn Warren has a marvelous skill at reproducing the vulgar idiom and hoe-handle ways of thinking, this writing is racy and authentic. Besides Ashby, Private Porsum (a local hero utilized by Bogan) and a wit named Duckfoot Drake are admirably drawn, but because their detailed stories contribute only in a collateral way to our sense of the cold, scaly monster who is Bogan Murdock, they increase the diffusion which is the tale's greatest weakness. Like the victim of a street accident, rather than the demon of the fatal car, Mr. Warren's monstrous protagonist is obscured by the crowd.

Because *At Heaven's Gate* was a failure, despite the lavishment upon it of unusual knowledge of the craft of fiction and of no small skill, *All the King's Men* is an impressive and important book. Warren has again chosen to portray the monster by indirection, by his effect on other people, but this time he has realized that all the persons in the novel must contribute to his central character, in this instance a state boss named Willie Stark, who bears a close resemblance to the chief benefactor of the University of Louisiana when Warren was on its faculty—Huey Long. All the characters in the novel, even the three very different women who worship Willie Stark, are truly the "King's 'men.'" He commands their souls as well as their bodies, and each is a separate mirror reflecting like a housefly's eyes the enormity which is Willie Stark. Even if Mother Goose avers that "all the King's men couldn't put Humpty-Dumpty together again," Robert Penn Warren comes very close to making them do it in this novel, for Willie is not only a plausible embodiment of the qualities which made the notorious "Kingfish" succeed in Louisiana, but he is also the most omnivorous monster that the author has drawn. Unlike Bogan Murdock, Willie Stark is no wire-puller; he is out in the middle of the stage, willing to gouge and bite, daring all comers, cynically acknowledging his take in graft, but asserting that the return of his machine to the sovereign people is larger than that yielded up by any other political organization. Willie is a demagogue, he is an unconscionable rogue, he is a smooth scoundrel, he is a beast; but he is closer to the people than their previous genteel rulers have been, and he is able to make them believe that he is their "pal," somehow frustrate in his large intent to better their circumstances. Willie was a good boy originally—a country lawyer, married to a schoolteacher, whom the city bosses took up to split an opponent's vote; when he learned the use he was being put to, Willie came of age. He drove out of politics those who had used him or made them like Tiny Duffy, his fearful tools. But as "The Boss" he still has something about him (in Warren's eyes) that suggests the perspiring young man who was disappointed to find that the country school he had helped to build was made of rotten brick. Tough and cynical, he has not quite smothered in himself, allegedly, that which was toothsomely tender to his first exploiters. Perception of this makes him a strange anomaly to the reader, perhaps, but Willie Stark's prototype won and maintained his power because he was some sort of anomaly. So far as portrayal of Willie Stark is his object, Warren is nearer to the realist than to the caricaturist: His demagogue is a more plausible monster than Sinclair Lewis' Berzelius Windrip or Dos Passos' Chuck Crawford.

All the King's Men, however, is not wholly Willie Stark's story. The journalist-narrator of the tale, Jack Burden, claims the story as his story; and, gauged by the simple tests of space and emphasis, his claim is justified. Burden had a hand in the making of Willie Stark. Together with Sadie Burke, a pock-marked Irish girl who had been using her brains and her body to make a living on the fringe of politics, he had given Willie the tip-off which had redirected his career. Willie rewarded Sadie by making her his secretary and mistress; Jack became the Harry Hopkins of the Stark regime, lending advice, "yessing" the Boss, doing "research" on people who gave his master trouble.

By the formulas of the Deep South, Jack Burden of Burden's Landing is an aristocrat. He comes from a great house, set in a row of great houses, among live oak and magnolia trees, where his boyhood companions were Anne and Adam Stanton, children of the governor, and where his counselor was the respected Judge Irwin. But the house of Burden is a decaying house, and more than the Jew has squat on the window sill. His father has deserted his mother, that lady has had a sequence of husbands, and Jack himself, too apathetic to woo Anne Stanton, has drifted in and out of matrimony with a puzzled blonde. The downward pull of gravity took him into journalism after he had dabbled with law and research in history. Service to Willie Stark provides him with the melodrama which his jaded senses seem to require. He never sees himself as an actor in that melodrama but always as an aloof and amused spectator.

The melodrama, however, encompasses Jack Burden — and in a way to suggest that Warren would like to throw Polti at the reader. A "research" job for Willie on Judge Irwin drives Jack's boyhood counselor to suicide but wrings from Jack's mother the admission that the Judge was Jack's real father and the only man she had ever loved. In the process of forcing Adam Stanton, who has become a famous surgeon, to serve as head of the hospital that Willie Stark is building, Jack Burden discovers that Anne Stanton—who has remained the heroine of his reveries—is one of Willie's mistresses. An atomic denouement resolves the plot. Willie's football-hero son breaks his back in a game; Adam Stanton saves the boy's life, but he will be paralyzed. The event decides Willie to return to Lucy Stark, the schoolteacher mother of the boy; and Sadie Burke, who sees that she cannot escape the consequences of Willie's reformation, causes his assassination by revealing to Adam through Tiny Duffy that Willie has corrupted his sister. After firing two shots into Willie, Adam is instantly slain by one of the Boss's gunmen; Willie himself, however, lingers for several days, long enough to tell Jack, "It might have been all different. . . . You got to believe that"; and apparently Jack believes. He, too, experiences some sort of reformation, for at the end of the novel he is tarrying briefly in the house Judge Irwin had left him, with his supposititious father as his pensioner and with Anne Stanton as his bride.

Faced with the problem of making Willie's influence all pervasive, Warren endows Jack with a respect for his Boss that survives his own discovery of contrition, a contrition signalized by his taking the somewhat soiled Anne Stanton to his bosom. Jack is really convinced a great change has come in himself:

> The change did not happen all at once. . . . There was a time when he came to believe that nobody had any responsibility for anything. . . . [This] gave him a sort of satisfaction, because it meant that he could not be called guilty of anything, not even of having squandered happiness or having killed his father, or of having delivered his two friends into each other's hands and death. [Later he came to the view that although Adam Stanton, "the man of idea," and Willie Stark, "the man of fact," were the doom of each other, both had] lived in the agony of will. . . . [God is the author of evil], for it would have been a thing of trifling and contemptible ease for Perfection to create mere perfec-

tion. . . . That had to be so that the creation of good [with God's help] might be the index of man's power and glory.

That is, Jack Burden has moved allegedly from a purely naturalistic to a Christian point of view, albeit heretical on the problem of evil. When Burden was Willie's hench-man, he was a sinuous moral monster, perhaps eclipsing his master; the question now is: What change has really taken place in him? He condones Willie on the ground that, given a longer lease on life, Willie would have become an angel of light. That is, chance defeated Willie. But a world where caprice rules is not a world in which the human will can rear goodly structures. It is a world of facile excuses, of human monsters. The confusion of Jack Burden—who certainly is still a warped creature at the end of *All the King's Men*—explains why the monsters of Robert Penn Warren, and the monsters of other writers, have only entertainment value, have no moral purport. Villains by an old-fashioned standard, they are no longer villainous; they are only the "erring pals" of the "erring" Jack Burdens. Monsters seen through a crooked lens are distorted in the direction, apparently, of perfection. By stressing the imper-fections of everyone, the novelist diminishes the mon-strousness of the major rascals. Perhaps it is impossible to do otherwise than to caricature the monster if moral indignation is to be retained. Robert Penn Warren, specialist in monsters, has steadily produced more plau-sible ones, but with waning indignation. The monsters of Dos Passos and Sinclair Lewis are not plausible, but *Number One* and *It Can't Happen Here* have the right instinct. Is it possible in any way to condone the Huey Longs? Macaulay thought it was no excuse for Charles I that he was a good husband and father.

AFTERWORD

This essay was among the earliest written on the fiction of Robert Penn Warren. Later criticism has empha-sized Warren's absorption with the evils of monomaniacal obsession, with fanatical absolutism, not so apparent when this was written. It is clearer now that he has resurrected a kind of perverted and musty Calvinism, in which all men are corrupt or corruptible, but those who come to a recognition of their evil are the better fellows. This would cover Jack Burden who, in Warren's eyes, appears redeemed through self-knowledge at the end of the novel, but who seems to me so corrupt, so much a villain, that I doubt his facile redemption. The clearest treatment of the theme is in the scabrous poem *Brother to Dragons* in which Jefferson is lessoned out of his allegedly complete faith in man through the mad behavior of a relative.

The chief fault of this essay, which concentrates on Mr. Warren's avidity for monsters and villainy, is that it does not do what it sets itself to do, attempt an explanation for the author's own obsession. One cannot but note how much his fictions, and especially his long poem, resemble the early verse narratives of Conrad Aiken in their penchant for rhetoric, melodrama, universal corruption, and contrapuntal realism. Might a common explanation fit both men? Becoming acquainted with the work of Jean-Paul Sartre since this essay was written, I see in Sartre's discussion of anguish explanation enough of Warren's motivation—like Aiken, and possibly Poe, he is an alienated writer, perhaps the most alienated of our times, whether an artist in the backcountry South or a Southerner living in Connecticut. Alienation would explain all of the outrages against good taste—indecency, obscenity, vulgarity—that appear in the creative work of Warren, but are absent from his criticism, which is markedly formal. The latter, however, is addressed to academicians, a society which has accepted Warren and which he can accept. Warren's position is especially interesting, for beyond satisfying their formulas, he partially anticipates the existentialists in many ways.

i Hart Crane and His Friends

It is to be hoped that the publication in paper-backs within the year of *The Complete Poems of Hart Crane* and of Philip Horton's admirable biography will arouse in a new generation of readers something of the enthusiasm for Crane's poetry which existed in the late twenties, but which was savagely extinguished at the beginning of the next decade. To be sure, Crane himself made an almost fatal error when he forsook the papal immunity that discipleship to Mr. Eliot had previously provided him and, in signing off, designated his former mentor a "religious gunman." This not wholly inapplicable epithet had the scent of a man in it, and the wolf pack found the carcass that Crane himself had thought to bury in the deep. They had his blood, and his liver and his lights, and only fragments of him got embalmed in anthologies, giving further force to the declaration of his assassins that Crane was "only a fragmentary poet or poet of fragments" anyway. They should know—they tore him to bits.

Many readers who have known Hart Crane only piece-meal or not at all (the original edition of *The Complete Poems*, compiled by Waldo Frank in 1933, has long been out of print) will be possessed by the soaring imagination of the whole design of *The Bridge*; will find that *Voyages* is six poems, not one; and will read a score of other brilliantly executed poems never anthologized. The freshly initiated reader, led to Philip Horton's *Hart Crane*, will discover in it one of the most understanding studies ever made of tortured genius. Dispassionate presentation of as bad a parentage as a man ever had made it unnecessary for Horton to gloss over either Crane's alcoholism or his homosexuality; the clouds stand, but through them shine the true gifts of the poet. If the poet's reputation is at all recoverable, the merits of this hitherto unobtainable biography, written twenty years ago and forgotten with its repudiated subject, may be realized again. The modest paper presentation of both books augurs well for new readers unaffected by the critical abuse heaped on Crane before his death in 1932.

It is an unpleasant historical fact that the assault upon the *corpus* of Crane was led by two lesser poets whom he had counted as his friends: Yvor Winters and Allen Tate. Nothing is gained by exploring their motivation, but something might be salvaged for Hart Crane by noting the nature and limits of the attack and what remains of the poetry beyond its scope. *The Bridge* is Crane's masterwork, and the attack is concentrated almost entirely upon it: Tate finds fault with the poem's substance and symbolism; Winters, with its structure.

Tate writes, "If we subtract from Crane's idea its periphery of sensation, we have left only the dead abstraction, the Greatness of America, which is capable of elucidation neither on the logical plane nor in terms of a generally accepted idea of America." Now, as we know from the letters to Otto Kahn, and as Allen Tate knew from Crane's letters to him, *The Bridge* was constructed on the analogy of a symphony. Who would think of "subtracting" from a symphony "its periphery of sensation"? Yet that is precisely what Tate does and he is left with an abstract idea which he affirms is "the Greatness of America," an impossible idea—for a *symphony?* Anton Dvorak and *The New World Symphony* would have fared very badly had Allen Tate been in Henry Krehbiel's or James Huneker's shoes. It is gratuitous after this, surely, to belabor Hart Crane for lacking "indispensable understanding" of America; like Charles Beard, according to Mr. Tate, he has only "information" about it.

But the theme of *The Bridge* is *not* "the Greatness of

America," as Tate assumes, but the instinctive aspiration of America toward universal love—a theme good enough for any aspiring symphonic structure, such as Brooklyn Bridge, with its "choiring strings," to symbolize:

> Of stars Thou art the stitch and stallion glow
> And like an organ, Thou, with sound of doom—
> Sight, sound and flesh Thou leadest from time's realm
> As love strikes clear direction for the helm.

This passage, found in "Atlantis," the last section of the poem but the first written, is clearly led up to throughout, giving the whole composition a unity that is not allowed by those who have misread it.

As for symbolism, Crane's use of which Tate terms "Irrational," the most offensive example to Tate is that of the subway in the section called "The Tunnel." "There is no reason," says Mr. Tate, "why the subway should be a fitter symbol of damnation than the aeroplane: both were produced by the same mentality on the same moral plane." This gem of criticism may properly be taken as symbolic of the mental plane on which the whole analysis of *The Bridge* has been conducted. The Bridge, whose "curveship lends a myth to God," leads men out of "time's realm" in the last section of the poem; this symbolism is matched in the previous section, "The Tunnel," by a "counter-curveship" which traverses hell, as the poet, self-identifying with Edgar Allan Poe, proceeds under the East River to Brooklyn. It's as simple as that.

Before writing *The Bridge*, Crane had discovered a principle of organization from his study of Rimbaud which he extended from the synesthetic metaphor ("cloudy clinch of bandy eyes") to elements of structure. He condemned in his poem *For the Marriage of Faustus and Helen* those who had not the imagination to structure by opposites as well as by identicals:

> There is a world dimensional
> for those untwisted by the
> love of things irreconcilable . . .

The attacks upon the structure of *The Bridge* have all come from those operating in "the world dimensional"; if the principle of opposites were applied, as it has just been applied to the last two sections of the poem, *The Bridge* would have a unity denied it. Mr. Winters makes a travesty of Crane's decent modesty by using statements from his personal letters to indicate that the poet was not himself conscious of any unifying principle; in the tightest place, he does hit with only a superficial glance at the poem itself: "When Crane was putting the sequence into final order, he wrote me that he wanted to include the [three] songs because he liked them, but that he was not sure the inclusion would be justified."

The "Three Songs," constituting Section IV of *The Bridge*, are "Southern Cross," "National Winter Garden," and "Virginia." Even in Winters' inadequate and inaccurate description of them, these three poems are related to one another through the principle of musical counterpoint and are variants upon the main theme of *The Bridge*: "Southern Cross" is "a kind of love poem addressed to the constellation . . . as if the constellation were . . . a female divinity"; "National Winter Garden" is "a vision of love as lust"; and "Virginia" is a "slight and casual vision of sentimental love in the city." It would seem that Hart Crane found a way to integrate the lyrics in his structure. Organically the group occupies an identical place with the single lyric used by Eliot in *The Waste Land* and in each of the *Four Quartets*.

There exists no adequate examination of *The Bridge*; but if it were studied as a symphonic composition, rather than as an "epic" (the term Tate repeatedly applies to it, despite his knowledge of the author's intention), and if the author's original principles were kept in mind, it would be found to be a genuine poem of a high order, as carefully developed as it is enriched with vivid metaphor. There exists only casual and passing treatment of Crane's other poetry. He was able to impart something of the eternal restlessness of the sea to his descriptive verses without the aid of imitative metre, such as Southey and Longfellow used. Disheartened by Winters' obtuseness to his effects, he remarked that someone should buy the latter a cruise. In *Faustus and Helen* he had seen the face that launched a thousand ships in the features of a homebound working girl on a Brooklyn trolley. Pressing this principle of social opposites (Faustus was the son of a wealthy candy manufacturer) Hart Crane wrote some of the most sympathetic as well as the most imaginative lyrics of his generation. Consider "Black Tambourine," "The Idiot," and "Stark Major." Or consider, in the subjective mood, "A Postscript," set at the end of his verses:

> *Friendship agony! words came to me*
> *At last shyly. My only final friends—*
> *the wren and thrush, made solid print for me*
> *across dawn's broken arc. . . .*

ii The "Unfractioned Idiom" of The Bridge

Hart Crane's Sanskrit Charge: A Study of "The Bridge," by L. C. Dembo, is, I think, the bravest effort in recent criticism. With such critics as Malcolm Cowley, Allen Tate, Yvor Winters, F. O. Matthiessen, and R. P. Blackmur arrayed against him, Mr. L. C. Dembo has undertaken to prove the unity and artistic completeness of *The Bridge.* If ever the accent were on youth it is here—Dembo belongs to a generation that has had no personal contact with the poet and has not suffered, nor has friends who have suffered, from the intemperate nature of the most unstable genius of the twenties. There is no blur between Dembo and the object of his contemplation: he writes solely about Crane's masterpiece—in fact, his is the only extensive essay in which there is scarcely an allusion to the unhappy career of the poet. Dembo's concentration, his objectivity, has paid off; for *The Bridge* emerges clearly as an artistic whole, challenging comparison with the best-conceived long poems of our era.

It is Dembo's thesis that Crane was powerfully influenced by Nietzsche's *The Birth of Tragedy*, and he does something substantial in showing that much of Crane's early poetry is a product of "unreconciled" Apollonian and Dionysian impulses. In *For the Marriage of Faustus and Helen*, however, Dembo sees these impulses first reconciled, and the pattern of that poem, with adumbration and enlargement, is transferred to *The Bridge*. Through dream, which supplies the poet with symbolism, notably that of Pocahontas as the rich American earth; through meditation, which includes contemplation of the realities of the modern world, bringing only despair; and finally, through reaffirmation of faith in despair, the "tragic" poet arrives in "Atlantis" at the Apollonian state of ecstasy where he can enjoy his "oneness with the primal source of the universe." It is in this Nietzschean sense that *The Bridge* is "a symbolic dream picture" and not simply a naïve myth of the greatness of America. The passages of despair are essential to the ecstasy.

Probably in his desire to emphasize the unity of the poem Dembo bears down a little too hard on his special conception of Crane as a "tragic" poet, leaving a false impression that Nietzsche was his sole guide in composition. It is quite as easy to show that Eliot, an influence on Crane's early poetry, was influential with *The Bridge* as well, without damage to the thesis of the poem's unity. "My work for the past two years," Crane told Munson in 1923, ". . . has been more influenced by Eliot than any other modern," yet when *The Waste Land* appeared he pronounced it "damned dead." Eliot, he believed, "ignored certain spiritual . . . possibilities as real and powerful now as . . . in the time of Blake," and he resolved to make him "a point of departure." That departure is as much signalized by the spiritual hope and triumph of *The Bridge* as anything; yet the symphonic form of Crane's poem was probably built on the analogy to the Beethoven quartet, which Eliot had used in *The Waste Land*, in which the lyric section "Death by Water" became permissive to the "Three Songs" without damage to the musical unity of the composition. The mark of Eliot is on such lines as "Behind / My father's cannery works I used to see / Rail-squatters ranged in nomad raillery" (compare: "While I was fishing . . . round behind the gashouse / Musing . . . on the king my father's death"), but more importantly upon the water passages which suture the poem and symbolize not death, as Dembo seems to think, but vibrant hope:

> High unto Labrador the sun strikes free
> Her speechless dream of snow, and stirred again
> She is the torrent and the singing tree;
> And she is virgin to the last of men. . . .

Though Dembo cites a number of passages plainly imitative of Whitman, he carefully avoids admitting that Whitman was as great an influence as Nietzsche on *The Bridge*, for the simple reason that "critics such as Winters have altogether too easily identified Crane with Whitman." He would have done better, I believe, to have justified Crane's use of Whitman, for the confidence Crane imposes in America and in democracy could hardly have originated with Nietzsche. Dembo will not go this far: "*The Bridge*," he writes, "is not concerned with America in the same way that *Leaves of Grass* is: it does not even pretend to work out a faith in 'Democracy'." I believe this defensive—and unsound. It misinterprets the poet who uses "Love" wherever Dembo strangely refers to "the Absolute" (Love of whom?—"us lowliest," I assume) and who confides "My hand in yours, Walt Whitman." Admirably as Dembo does in placing "Three Songs" in the design of the whole poem, he misses the *Crescendo* in the section when he says that the third song "Virginia" presents "the third fallen image of Pocahontas." Not so; she is the virgin and redeemed image of the three, a girl from Woolworth's (symbolized by the "nickel-dime tower" and "the high wheat tower"—see the carvings on the Woolworth Building) whom Crane idealizes as he does that other shop girl in "Faustus and Helen." Why, otherwise, would he call her "Cathedral Mary"?

These are differences, however, that merely strengthen Mr. Dembo's case. I rejoice in Dembo's book, for it beckons in an era in which Hart Crane will get his just due as one of the three great original poets of the renascence of the twenties, the three most likely to survive—Eliot, Crane, and Wallace Stevens, in that order. Of course, much more work will have to be done on him, especially in showing what Rimbaud, Laforgue, and Blake contributed, and in interpreting the telescoped imagery; but Dembo has opened the way.

AFTERWORD

The critic who never gives expression to decent wrath is no critic at all—he is one of the unnatural compromises of nature, a female transvestite, a scribbling hermaphrodite. I do not repent me of "Hart Crane and His Friends," despite the pain I may have inflicted, for someone's pain attends every birth and I hoped that out of agony and wrath—if I give pain, I also share it—a higher respect for Hart Crane as a poet would be born. I trusted that the cries at parturition would attract better physicians, better critics, than I to the study of Crane's poetry; hence my delight in Mr. Dembo's sympathetic and understanding critique. But the unexpected also happened. Robert Lowell read my defense of *The Bridge* and it inspired, so he told Macha Rosenthal, then Poetry Editor of *The Nation*, that glorious, heartfelt poem, "Words for Hart Crane," contributed to that periodical and later reprinted in *Life Studies*. I take these auguries to mean that Hart Crane will come into his own with a younger generation.

The history of reception, biographical fact, structural analysis, and *explication de texte* go into the two review-essays, for I use the Dembo review deliberately to strengthen my argument as to the unity of *The Bridge*. But on the theme of universal love, so persistently held to by the poet, I might have profitably brought into the discussion a poetic reiteration of Crane's intent in "The Broken Tower," written in Taxco, just before his fatal voyage. In this poem Crane rejoices that he has been permitted to be the "sexton slave" to the matin bells ("Deity's young name [is] Love"), that is, Crane is definitely referring to *The Bridge* in "my word I poured," but wonders, thinking of his own abnormal practices, his lusts ("the steep encroachments of my blood"), if his music is as "pure," as worthy, as that of the bells. His answer to the doubt that possessed him, and had possessed him since the reception of *The Bridge*, he resolves by finding his answer (as stated in the last three stanzas) in the present love of Peggy Baird, which sustained him almost to his "final nihilistic act."

I rejoice in the news that Mr. R. W. B. Lewis, of Yale University, is working on a critical study of Crane's poetry. I wish, though he has told me how much he disagrees with me, Mr. Malcolm Cowley would put in print his view of the circumstances that attended the publication of *The Bridge*.

BY RAILING AT "our sympathy for the underdog" during the great depression Robert Frost did himself permanent harm, and all of Ernest Hemingway's sportsmanship is called into question by his having twitted Sinclair Lewis on his fiery complexion when the man was ill with skin cancer. Yet with an immunity unequalled, Mr. T. S. Eliot has abused and insulted whole peoples and races. Indeed, the general critical evasion of his early bigotry raises the question if his numerous adulators have not consciously or unconsciously, shared in it. That question is seriously pointed up when Eliot himself, though he has suffered no real public reproof, flinches from approval of things in his early poetry which have begun to fill him with distaste, if not contrition.

Unfortunately the passage in which the poet braces himself against the silly adulation he has received has been more completely ignored, even more than his early offenses. In "Little Gidding," in the role of a fire warden during a bombing raid, which makes his spot in wartime England resemble the Purgatory of Dante, he meets a prophetic ghost, reminiscent of Arnaut Daniel, who describes the three-fold chastisement which will come to him with age. He will know the bafflement of dulling sense (always an important matter to Eliot), the futility of railing at folly, and, presumably the worst of punishments—

> . . . *the shame*
> *Of motives late revealed, and the awareness*
> *Of things ill-done and done to others' harm*
> *Which once you took for exercise of virtue.*
> *Then fools' approval stings, and honour stains.*

There is no difficulty at all with this passage if one assumes that it applies to Eliot's creative work, for in a comparatively inactive life there is little else that he has done to solicit anyone's judgment. As an "exercise of virtue" his church activities are not the ones here indicated since they could hardly have done others harm and since they are still an enduring commitment. If the reference to "things ill-done and done to others' harm" is looked for in the poetry, however, Eliot's meaning is abundantly clear: he refers to the abusive verses in which the most bestial and vulgar Irish, Jews, and Cockneys are made symbolic of their kind.

The more difficult line to understand is the one in which Eliot refers to these offensive verses as an "exercise of virtue." The difficulty may be dissipated if we will but consider the relations the poet had with the despised and reprobated people in his impressionable youth. If it were only humorous contempt that Eliot had expressed, the Keith circuit, and vaudeville generally, of which Eliot was fond, could be blamed for his attitudes; there the Irish, the Jew, and the Cockney were commonly ridiculed, the actors themselves often being pandering representatives of their kind, but still wonderfully good entertainers.

A Harvard man of the class of '10, however, had little reason to be amused by the Irish off the stage—a feud existed between the young toughs of Boston and the undergraduates of Cambridge which made it unwise for a college boy to venture across the Charles after dark unless he went with a band of his fellows and carried a stick. In Eliot's Harvard experience, therefore, there might have been grounds for dislike of some Irishmen, though certainly not grounds for a virulent hatred of the whole race.

But shortly an already-prejudiced Eliot was given stronger reasons for hating the Irish. He had transferred his person and his loyalties to England in a deeply emotional way. Eighteen months after he had established himself there and while the British were struggling for survival on the Continent against the superior weight of the Kaiser's divisions, the Irish Rebellion broke out, aided and abetted by some slight, but then exaggerated, German help. To a young Anglophile, contemplating the bloody Easter riots and later outrages, it was only the expression of virtuous indignation to repudiate Emerson's definition of history as "the lengthened shadow of a man" with the awful figure of Sweeney straddling in the morning sun. The motivation seems as obvious as the symbolism, and perhaps the unforgivable thing is not so much the writing of the pieces as the keeping of them alive in edition after edition.

It is almost axiomatic that a man who wins support for his prejudices intensifies and broadens their scope. The earliest Sweeney poem was published in 1918; "Burbank with a Baedeker: Bleistein with a Cigar," the first of the anti-Semitic poems, appeared in the summer of 1919; and the following year Eliot chose to lead off the British edition of his collected poems *Ara Vos Prec* with it and with "Gerontion"—which make the "Jews" and international bankers responsible for the decline of Western culture. It is hard to say whether Eliot came directly to this Spenglerian idea or whether he was led to it by Ezra Pound, who became a more violent, if less vivid expounder of it. One is inclined to suspect Eliot as the initiator because of his better knowledge of German and his visit to that country, as well as his growth and employment in what is too commonly the atmosphere of prejudice—his father was a businessman in St. Louis, where the German Jew has for a long time been eminently successful, and Eliot himself had been unhappily employed in a London bank in which the Rothschilds had been hated for a century. But the direction is, after all, of relatively little moment; Pound and Eliot were sunk in a common depravity while achieving a common brilliance and a very wide reputation.

Disapprobation of the Cockney brought up the train in

The Waste Land with its derisive portraits of Lil, her false friend Lou, Albert, Bill, Mrs. Porter and her daughter. Contempt of the vulgar always has the appearance of virtue, yet Eliot seems to display a gross appetite for it. If one's purpose were Freudian, one could make a pretty thesis out of the obvious attraction and repulsion to the poet of some of the sharpest details in the poems exhibiting his prejudices.

About 1920, when he was still engrossed in making capital out of those prejudices, Eliot became interested in religion. Poems like "A Cooking Egg" and "The Hippopotamus" had previously displayed a scarcely reverent approach to sacred matters. Possibly when Eliot chose to consider how much of a "traditionalist" he was, he had to take some account of that most traditional of all subjects, religion. At any rate, it is in "Whispers of Immortality," which contrasts the traditional attitude toward death of Dr. John Donne with the allurement of the flesh, as represented by Grishkin, that Eliot discovers how little energy his generation has "to keep our metaphysics warm." It is but a step, though a positive one, to what I take to be the theme of *The Waste Land*—that, since the true religion cannot be achieved in our time, it would be well to adopt the humanist code of "give, sympathize, and control."

"Gerontion," though published first, was written after *The Waste Land* was fully conceived. It differs religiously from the longer work in that it is a sectarian poem. But sectarianism, generally looked upon as divisive by the modern mind, is a sturdy crutch for those who, desiring faith, need help beyond themselves: it provides formulas and examples. So far as his poetry is concerned, the "Ariel Poems" and *Ash Wednesday* express the relief Eliot felt in reaching for this particular crutch.

Even in poems that may be designated sectarian there is a note of humility, painful self-abnegation, and self-scrutiny, which indicates the poet's concern with more than the formulas of religion. The personal examination suggested by *Ash Wednesday* must have led Eliot to the conclusion that bigotry is a very troublesome baggage for one seeking a more elevated spiritual ground. The first fruit of this discovery was the abandoning of work upon, and suppression of the unpublished parts of, *Sweeney Agonistes,* that "Aristophanic melodrama," which, despite its bias, is one of the most brilliantly conceived projects of the poetic renascence. We know that more of this play once existed than the two fragments which have been published, for the poet supplied Hallie Flanagan with a short concluding scene for her production of the sequence under the title, "Now I Know Love," in the Vassar Experimental Theatre in 1933. Since here is proof that the poet had the play outlined in his mind, that it has not been published or completed can only be a matter of deliberate choice. It would seem that the poet refused to carry further the maligning of a people however much the work would redound to his credit on another score.

But unfortunately this evidence is not conclusive, save to those who feel the sincerity of the poet's profession of Christian submission in *Ash Wednesday.* If one were hostile to Eliot, however, one might argue that the poet abandoned work on *Sweeney Agonistes* because he thought it inexpedient to complete it; by the thirties the popular temper had changed and Eliot might have feared the general indignation which has not come to him. As late as 1941 quite a case could have been strung together to support this point of view, but it would have to be based on old and repudiated things, not on new creations.

"Little Gidding" was published in *The New English Weekly* on October 15, 1942, and appeared in book form early in December of that year. The passage cited in this essay, however it may be evaluated as an act of contrition, is at least an expression of regret for injury done to others and of distaste for whatever approval the offending lines and poems have given. It must be accepted, however vague and indefinite, as a public confession of error. Under no obligation to accept it on the terms of the faith to which Mr. Eliot subscribes, we may evaluate it: 1] in terms of what it cost its author, 2] in relation to the context in which it appears, and 3] in terms of the justice which it does to those whom Eliot had injured. It should be strictly noted that Eliot himself indicates a desire for an evaluation by his contempt for "fools' approval"—which hits a good many living critics.

"Bow, stubborn knees," the King prays in *Hamlet* and one might fancy Eliot uttering the King's adjuration, for retraction has never been easy for him. Having condemned another poet early in his career, he does not say, "I was mistaken about him," but merely sets forth another opinion.

Declaring in *The Scared Wood* (1920) that Coleridge's metaphysical interest was "an affair of the emotions," Eliot dogmatically asserted, "But a literary critic should have no emotions except those immediately provoked by a work of art." However in the Preface to the *unrevised* 1928 edition, he says that his own interest is now in "the relation of poetry to the spiritual and social life of its times and other times," and adds, "This book is logically and chronologically the beginning" of that interest—which most obviously it isn't. Retraction is almost impossible for Eliot; hence more weight should be put upon his lines of regret, perhaps, than upon the easy *mea culpa* of another.

The lines appear, importantly, in the most mystical and devout poem of that religious group which makes up *Four Quartets*. "Little Gidding" is devoted to the subject of Spiritual Love, here symbolized by fire—fire which may weave a purgatorial garment of flame. Hence the passage has not merely the character of an expression of regret but it also has the severe intention of high atonement. His medium considered, Eliot could not be more grieved about his sins or more contrite in his confession of them. The tone and level of the composition forbid it. In their context, they are perfect.

But, the reader may fairly ask, is not the choice of context a deliberate evasion of the duty of specific and open public retraction? And one must answer reluctantly, yes. "Burbank with a Baedeker: Bleistein with a Cigar" and "Sweeney Erect" were unveiled affronts, specific in their language and vicious in their intent. Retraction of them should be in unmistakable terms, as categorical and complete as those of the original injury. Religion, and in particular Mr. Eliot's accepted faith, may not require this (I do not know and am indifferent), but the very code which Mr. Eliot invokes demands it. "Honour," now "stained," demands it.

AFTERWORD

Much as I have tried always to avoid it, I find that moral reproof sometimes creeps subtly into what I write. Despite the dreadful ukase, "Judge not lest ye be judged," surely framed with critics in mind, the American critic with a long Protestant heritage, finds himself in the forbidden territory, not infrequently unaware of how he got there. The ukase justifies the contempt of creative writers (now his nearest gods) for him, even though they must know that without him and his kind they would have no viable meaning. But there are occasions, certainly rare today, when the examination of an artist's morals and beliefs seem thoroughly justified. If an artist lessons the world about him, does he not expose himself to his own lessons? Yes, if we can also accord him respect for what lies above and beyond this lessoning. To look with a hard eye at those two magnificent poems, "Burnt Norton" and "Little Gidding," the finest metaphysical poems since the seventeenth century (I am quite aware of *The Hound of Heaven*), strikes the looker as the foulest *lèse-majesté*; he ought to cover his eyes from blinding. What so fine as that apostrophe to Love with which "Burnt Norton" closes? Yet what so niggardly as those lines of contrition, despite the poem's own vision of purgation by fire, in "Little Gidding"? Should we not expect something nobler in a sovereign poet? Grover Smith thinks I may have reached Eliot and teases me with Mrs. Carghill and her number, "It's Not Too Late for You to Love Me," in *The Elder Statesman*, but I'm hardly convinced. "Human kind cannot bear too much reality."

IT IS TIME we recognized that the so-called "New Poetry" movement in America ended nearly fifteen years ago with the outbreak of World War II and that reputations made since that date have little in common with earlier reputations. They lack, for example, the strong ingredient of popular approval. No poet who has emerged since 1940 is known the way Lindsay and Sandburg, Frost and Eliot, Robinson and Millay were known a decade before. Indeed, no current poet has won a public indorsement comparable to that which either Conrad Aiken or Elinor Wylie achieved in the twenties, neither of whom was ever regarded as a popular poet. Amy Lowell or Edgar Lee Masters, when each enjoyed a vogue, could have cast into undecipherable oblivion with their shadows the whole shoal of recent poets. Yet this remains to be said, despite their once considerable following, the poets of the "New Poetry" movement have no longer secure reputations: no one voluntarily reads Sara Teasdale, Masters, "H. D.," Miss Lowell, or Stephen Benét any more, Aiken and Miss Wylie are about as much respected as the adultery laws in New York, and Lindsay and Sandburg are condescended to. It remains to be seen if Lawrance Thompson's recent judicious selection of Robinson's poetry in *Tilbury Town* will stay the fading interest in that great poet's work; if not, only the reputations of Frost and Eliot—and we would add, of Wallace Stevens and William Carlos Williams—are what they once were. Pound has begun to be written off as a mere virtuoso, MacLeish as a rhetorician, and Hart Crane as an unintegrated ineffectual. Popular approval, the critics are saying, has nothing to do with the quality of verse. Perhaps without popular recognition current poets are writing better verse than their predecessors, and their day of proper acclamation will come. Donne lives—or, rather, has been revived. And Alexander Pope lurks behind the curtain awaiting a call.

There are factors, certainly, which make it much harder today to achieve a popular reputation than it was earlier in the twentieth century. One of these is the rise in printing costs. Who can afford a whole shelf of current poets at three and a half dollars a volume? There is only one class of individuals poorer than poetry lovers, and that is the poets themselves. We have a stupid tradition in America that poetry must be published on rag paper, watermarked and deckled, and bound like the memoirs of the mistress to a king, whereas newsprint and paper covers would be good enough—though this would frustrate the book-collectors, who are today expert gamblers in first editions and really the enemies of unpublished poets and poetry. The most notorious recent example of book-pricing is not some edition of six poems by e. e. cummings, notorious as those editions are, but the *Collected Poems of Conrad Aiken*, f.o.b. at over ten dollars! By returning frequently to the few book counters that display this volume and by surreptitious examination, I have discovered that Aiken has immeasurably improved as a poet since his *Selected Poems* were published in 1929. Poor Aiken! Who else is going to know this besides one or two millionaire collectors? Another and comparable evil to book-pricing is the rise in "permission" fees—those sums collected by publishers for the inclusion of a poet's work in anthologies, critical studies, and textbooks. Today a gathering of poetry like Monroe and Henderson's *The New Poetry* (1923), which contained around seven hundred poems in copyright, would be out of question for any publisher. Still more important, popular presentations of current verse, like Amy Lowell's *Tendencies in Modern American Poetry*

(1917) and Louis Untermeyer's *American Poetry since 1900* (1923), which quoted without charge a very considerable amount of poetry, including many whole poems, have been driven out of existence by permissions charges. In poetry circles anthology-makers and popularizers have long been ridiculed, but there is no denying that many a current poet would be better known today if he could have the assistance of an Untermeyer. Oscar Williams, hamstrung by permissions costs, is no such midwife to poetry as was he.

Finally, to draw a list of handicaps (which could be much extended) to a conclusion, current poets suffer from reaching maturity after a movement which still engages avid critical attention. The young critic has found that the quickest way to establish himself is to clarify a symbol or to explicate a line in Yeats and Eliot rather than to hazard everything by proclaiming his discovery of an unknown artist. Randall Jarrell's enthusiastic review of Robert Lowell's *Lord Weary's Castle* in the *Nation* is so rare an event today that it is much celebrated, but the critic who generously risked his own reputation for a neglected creative talent was common enough a generation ago. Think of Carl Van Doren, Harry Hansen, William Rose Benét, Christopher Morley, and the exceptionally generous "F. P. A." Mr. Van Doren almost single-handedly made the reputations of Elinor Wylie and E. A. Robinson. Explication is a dangerous and exciting exercise; it is an exercise of great value to the critic, despite the fact that the gentlemen I have just enumerated never consciously explicated a line; but the discovery and proclamation of a new poem of merit is still more dangerous and exciting, for it provides the test of battle. It would be a great day for poetry if several of the more talented young explicators would take an oath to elucidate nothing old until they had discovered something new. What a hush would fall over the New Criticism!

Leaving out of consideration the "Depression Poets," Gregory, Fearing, and Rukeyser, and the still fleeing "Fugitives," Allen Tate and Robert Penn Warren, whose

verse may properly be looked upon as terminating the
"New Poetry" movement despite the dissimilar aims of the
two camps, one finds an astonishingly large number of
writers who deserve consideration as poets—a larger number perhaps than would have engaged similar consideration in 1914. Their voices are pitched lower: modulation
and restraint have choked off the barbaric yawp, the
"kallyope yells," and the savage "boomlays." These poets
have purged their subject matter of sensationalism: no
grave dwellers rise from the mold to recite their tragedies;
hog butchers and the brawny truck handlers have disappeared; so also have the disintegrated fragments of the
cultures of past civilizations as the evidence of the decay of
ours. Their moods are witty, lyrical, and philosophical:
poetic tractarianism has vanished as completely as the
dramatic monologue. Current poets have adopted conventional meters and forms, and they use images and symbols
to strengthen the effect of the poem rather than to
browbeat the reader. Indeed, clarity seems a fairly universal aim with them. They have chosen, it would appear, to
discard practically all the devices by which the "New
Poetry" became a popular movement; concentrating on a
more absolute perfection they openly hazard achieving
only what Pound castigated as "the magazine touch" in
the belief that distinction within tested conventions is
more enduring than without. In an art where individuality
was the aim for a generation the pull toward classicism
would seem to have drawn all practitioners back into the
common mass. Yet the most conventional of forms is no
more conventional than the business suit, which is hardly a
handicap to our knowing and admiring or detesting the
man poured into it. When the hunger for poetry comes on
us, we will find the revived conventions no barrier to
distinguishing and appreciating what they convey.

Of the current poets, no two have pressed harder
toward conventionality in meter and form than Yvor
Winters and Richard Wilbur, both of whom depend
greatly on alternating rhymes, on rhymed couplets, and on
quatrains using only two rhymes. Winters even employs

inversion—so roundly condemned by the "New Poetry" movement:

> *Strong the scholar is to scan*
> *What is permanent in man. . . .*

Books, scholarship, and frequently teaching are Winters' subject matter—an area practically taboo to the previous generation but one in which he has worked with quiet skill and subdued passion. In this vein there is nothing better than his sonnet tribute, "To William Dinsmore Briggs Conducting His Seminar," and his digest into nine flawless quatrains of "Sir Gawaine and the Green Knight." The stoic suppression of feeling in the former poem must be sensed by every reader, but only those of us who heard Briggs lecture can appreciate the absolute aptness of the vivifying details that make the poem a perfect vignette as well as a tribute. "Sir Gawaine and the Green Knight" begins with a vigor it would seem impossible to maintain—"Reptilian green the wrinkled throat"—yet the poem does not fall away from its opening line; it would in fact require the greatest skill to surpass Mr. Winters' sense of the sinuous hold of the temptress on the knight, which he very effectively conveys. This is bookish poetry, but, if books are what we delight in, why should they not be the subject of poetry? Winters is in no sense chained to the scriptorium; he comes out of his cubicle to give us a California not got in Hollywood sequences or in Robinson Jeffers, a California of "persimmon, walnut, loquat, fig, and grape"; he comes out to speak of his young Airedale bitch lost in the salt marsh; and he comes furiously out in defense of his friend Roy Lamson, accused of murder, and in defense of academic liberty in his courageous "Ode on the Despoilers of Learning." Unlike so many of his contemporaries, Yvor Winters is not a wit, and he is dismal only when he attempts to be witty, epigrammatic, or cryptic.

With two slender volumes of verse, *The Beautiful Changes* (1947) and *Ceremony and Other Poems* (1950), Richard Wilbur has gained a prestige in his craft that

many might envy. No one since Landor has written such
quiet poetry. Poetry, Mr. Wilbur holds, is addressed only
to the Muse. "It is the one function of the Muse to cover
up the fact that poems are not addressed to anyone in
particular." Wilbur's titles are jaunty and patently derived
from Wallace Stevens: "Then," "Games One*" (the
asterisk is a part of the title), "Still, Citizen Sparrow,"
"He Was," "A Simile for Her Smile." Though he produces
at times a refinement on Stevens' whimsicality—

> *A ball will bounce, but less and less. It's not*
> *A light-hearted thing, resents its own resilience*

—his real forte is to imbue the apposite descriptive phrase
or image with expansible meaning. How rich his counsel to
Adam (or to Man) to take no further pride in his mental
development but to

> *Envy the gorgeous gallops of the sea*
> *Whose horses never know their lunar reins.*

All sorts of critical anxieties have been expressed about
Richard Wilbur because he has so much promise: Peter
Viereck, for example, hints that Wilbur may become too
"bland" ("He has all the qualities of a great artist except
vulgarity"), and Horace Gregory worries lest Wilbur
"suffer too much unthinking patronage"; but there seems
to be a consistent philosophy behind his writing which will
force its way through and impart virility to his verse. His
real problem is a minor one: to conceal some of the tricks
of his verse, like starting a new thought too frequently with
the last two syllables of a stanza—which has something of
the effect of a Hamiltonian gesture in elocution, so slick
that it is obvious. The perfectionist in Wilbur will take
care of this while the poet in him moves on to larger
themes, already hinted at in the magnificent "Speech for
the Repeal of the McCarran Act." Let us not forget that
he has pledged himself to "wit and wakefulness."

Though Theodore Roethke seems to have done violence
to the current ukase against novelty, it is a very gentle,
specious violence, for all that he has done is to lead us into

the unpoetized field of the greenhouse grower and the horticulturist. Roethke's poems, little verbal etchings, fall like seeds into soft ground. There is charm in pieces like "Child on Top of a Greenhouse" and "My Papa's Waltz," the latter an amusing picture of a slightly intoxicated gardener who, insisting on dancing with his small son, beats time upon his head "with a palm caked hard by dirt." Roethke's sensorium is particularly sharp, as nothing proves so well as "Root Cellar," yet one wonders if his verse will persist in having appeal for long; there is something about it that suggests the transciency of the Imagists, possibly because he chiefly conveys sense impressions.

Narrowness of scope eliminates from consideration many current poets, but it will never be a reason for not considering Delmore Schwartz, by all odds the most prolific and the most far-ranging of recent writers in his medium, save possibly Selden Rodman, who seems to have more connections with the "Depression Poets" than elsewhere. Unlike his fellows, Schwartz has not purged himself of exhibitionism, and many a fine poem is lost in volumes containing fantastic essays and capricious, unrelated narratives, as, for example, in *Vaudeville for a Princess* (1950). He is full of tricks, a favorite being to take a familiar line of verse and turn it into a poem with an ironic play upon the original:

> *When that I was and a little boy*
> *With a hey ho, the wind and the rain,*
> *I did not know the truth of joy,*
> *I thought that life was passed in pain.*

Schwartz springs too easily doglike after Hugh Wystan Auden, making his diction the popular argot, derisively burlesquing serious predecessors, playing Byronic, and twitching off syllables in his smoothest verse:

> *Poor Poe! and cursèd poets everywhere:*
> *Taught by their strict art to reject the eas-*
> *Y second-best, the well-known lesser good . . .*

Pucklike waggishness is a relief when the set is solemn, but who makes a diet of popcorn? If Delmore Schwartz, however, does not "think continually of those who are truly great," unless derisively, he knows also his own limitations and can equally well burlesque those. Picking up a phrase from Whitehead and writing of "the withness" of his body, he makes himself a clowning bear who

> *Howls in his sleep because the tight-rope*
> *Trembles and shows the darkness beneath.*

It will gradually come home to the unfamiliar reader of Schwartz, unless he stumbles at first upon "The Heavy Bear That Goes with Me" or "A Dog Named Ego, the Snowflakes as Kisses," that much of this poet's gaiety is forced, that it covers his despair that so much of life, as he says in his well-known aubade, "In the Naked Bed, in Plato's Cave," is "beginning again and again, while time is unforgiven."

When the New Directions annual *Five Young American Poets* produced both John Berryman and Randall Jarrell in 1940, the idea behind the venture seemed brilliantly vindicated. Berryman, however, has been a good deal diverted into criticism, and World War II seems to have done something to the talent of Jarrell. Yet it is much too early to despair of either. One cannot forget the insane clarity or the sardonic coolness with which Berryman touched world events in his debut—murder in Harlan, civil war in Spain, rape in Poland.

> . . . *A Spaniard learnt that any time is time*
> *For German or Italian doom.*

Though the same prose diction is employed in his later work, clarity has given way to turgidity as metaphor tumbles over metaphor and observation crowds upon observation, as in "New Year's Eve" and "The Dispossessed."

Randall Jarrell was hailed on his advent with almost as much enthusiasm as was Richard Wilbur later but with, I think, less justification, for he is not as severe a self-critic as Wilbur and far less a perfectionist. This is surprising, for he had declared at that time, "Winters is my *locus classicus*." But there was a looseness in some of his early work, a lack of precision and economy, too, which meant, with laxity, disaster later. When he was terse he was good, as in his description of the machine gun:

> *On the gunner's tripod, black with oil,*
> *Spits and gapes the pythoness.*

Could he have carried this vigor over into *Little Friend, Little Friend* (1945), which is largely made up of war poems, or more specifically Air Force poems, his reputation would be higher today; but he relaxed, depending, like Siegfried Sassoon, on the awfulness of his subject matter to create much of his effect. The result is a kind of versified tabloidism. We would say, however, that the man who could write "The Death of the Ball Turret Gunner," with its concentrated symbolism lifting it above mere journalism, is still to be reckoned with if we were not mindful of the admonition of Karl Shapiro, "How few successes lead our failures on."

John Ciardi, Karl Shapiro, and Robert Lowell all faced the allurements that the war provided and in different degrees rejected them for the more perdurable stuff of poetry. Of the three, Ciardi's rejection is the least positive, and his best work is still his war poetry. In this, however, there is no complete surrender to subject matter, but a witty and ironic commentary upon it, as in "Elegy Just in Case":

> *Here lie Ciardi's pearly bones*
> *In their ripe organic mess.*
> *Jungle blown, his chromosomes*
> *Breed to a new address.*

His sly literary allusions, his intellectualism, provide elements lacking in Jarrell's war poetry to give it tension (to use an abused word); Ciardi never descends into the bathos of Jarrell. If he can avoid being a mere wit (as in "Vale," of which he plainly thinks too much), he may be able to find an important new subject matter and claim it for his own. There is evidence that he is searching.

Karl Shapiro has conducted his own education in public. Though *Person, Place, and Thing* (1942) was instantly acclaimed, it is an inferior volume of poetry compared with his latest, *Trial of a Poet* (1947). There are many who do not think this, so many, in fact, that just recently David Daiches had to reaffirm Shapiro's importance. But the poems in *Person, Place, and Thing* by current standards lack finish or never should have been attempted; like those of Delmore Schwartz, they suggest Auden or Hart Crane. The vivid and much anthologized "The Fly" gets its vividness chiefly from its adjectives in such phrases as "polyhedral eye," "gluey foot," "tight belly," "amber muck," just as Auden once got effects chiefly from adjectives. Other poems, like "The Waitress," "Buick," and "Auto Wreck," remind one of the Rimbaud stage of Hart Crane's development. Only neglected poems, like "The Contraband," suggest current endeavors in poetry. *V-Letter and Other Poems* (1944) was better from the current point of view, in that stanzaic patterns more regularly emerge and the more sensational tricks of *Person, Place, and Thing* are abandoned. Adjectives really enhance the nouns they modify rather than suffocate them. For example, "The wind begins a *low* magnificat." Not this alone but a greater reverence for his craft makes *V-Letter* a quieter and more ponderable volume. Shapiro tries now to be faultlessly exact in his statements. "Elegy for a Dead Soldier" attributes no false dreams to him; a typical soldier, Shapiro's subject never questioned "the idea of gain" or "felt that peace was but a loan":

> He shed his coat
> And not for brotherhood, but for his pay.
> To him the red flag marked the sewer main.

There are two right ways of looking at *Essay on Rime* (1945) and one wrong. The wrong way is to regard it as a manifesto for the current poetry. Actually, poets like

Richard Wilbur and Robert Lowell have pushed beyond anything stated in *Essay on Rime*, which anyway contains more negation than affirmation. One right way of looking at this long poem is to see it as a review, or reconsideration, of past poetry, a taking of one's latitude and longitude, before setting one's course. As such, it was apparently a necessary and important public step in Shapiro's development. But in itself, *Essay on Rime* is an effort in criticism to be compared with Pope's *An Essay on Criticism*; Pope had at once the advantage and disadvantage of rhymed couplets; if they made some of his observations more memorable, they shaped those observations indubitably to the cranky smartness that the couplet encourages. Shapiro's limpid blank verse is conversational in character and judicious in effect. You may not care for some of his judgments (he is incredibly wrong on Eliot's *Quartets*), but they are marvelously turned:

> *When Whitman had the nation on his brain*
> *He served us ill, in my opinion; his leap*
> *Into the personal infinite, however,*
> *Saved him from drowning in his Susquehanna.*

Essay on Rime is better structured than *An Essay on Criticism*; it does, however, end weakly and apologetically—one indication of its tentative and speculative character.

The proof of the worth of this critical (or reflective) exercise is found in *Trial of a Poet*, in which the sixteen lyrical and autobiographical poems in the section entitled "Recapitulations" are the most finished poetry that Shapiro has written. There are melody and loveliness here that the poet has not produced before:

> *I was born downtown on a wintry day*
> *And under the roof where Poe expired;*
> *Tended by nuns my mother lay*
> *Dark-haired and beautiful and tired.*

Between these lyrics and the title piece, which is a medley of prose and verse, stands a section which would almost seem to belong to an earlier stage in the poet's development. Its subordinate position, however, shows that Shapiro is less satisfied with it than with the lyrics, yet he will only grudgingly surrender his past. *Trial of a Poet* is the first thing of Shapiro's to show strongly the influence of Eliot: the general design suggests the form of *Murder in the Cathedral* and the pattern of the lines the character of Eliot's dramatic or "applied" verse. It remains to be seen if this marks an advance in the poet's work; as an essay in morals it is excellent.

I have reserved the finest of the current poets, Robert Lowell, to the last. Here is a man from whose whole philosophy, if I understand it, I must dissent as a Yankee and the heir of the Pilgrims, but for whose art I have boundless admiration. To begin with, I cannot assent to such facile and hackneyed generalizations as "a New England town is death and incest." Of the same order is the frequent implication that the Bay State Puritans, while hypocritically seeking Jehovah, were thriftily bent chiefly on accumulating real estate. Protestantism no more produced capitalism (Weber and Lowell to the contrary) than did the very competent French abbots of the monasteries of the thirteenth century when the kings and knights were away on the crusades; Felix Gras has shown there are many kinds of capitalism, some going back to Babylon. These are the sort of revelations, more poorly phrased, that daring young instructors make to sophomores in the ivy colleges. Furthermore, Lowell himself takes, or seems to take, a rather masochistic delight in his special version of Yankee history; it is as if it were a bed of glass and spikes, the more sharp and terrible to enhance his suffering. It lends a drama to his position in his poetry that few others can avail themselves of. Henry Adams' "Prayer to the Virgin of Chartres" indicated the literary thrift of this long ago.

Yet every poem in *Lord Weary's Castle* (1946) and *The Mills of the Kavanaughs* (1951) is a good poem, and many of them are great. Robert Lowell has a mastery of technique that none of his fellows, save Richard Wilbur, possesses. In the title poem in the second volume he makes the open couplet run off as easily and unostentatiously as Karl Shapiro manages blank verse. As a vehicle for verse I have often compared this couplet in operation to the old-fashioned motorcycle, with an annoying *put-put* of rhyme every five feet; the metaphor falls to the ground completely with Mr. Shapiro's versification where one passes the rhyme without noticing it, as in a modern silent car. Further, there are no strained figures in his poetry and no pretentious collocations of words. Sonorousness is everywhere characteristic, with just enough variety to avoid monotony of pattern. In a trivial way, the war is in both books, but it is kept very much subordinate to other things. "The Exile's Return" touches swiftly the danger to occupation troops, "The Dead in Europe" mingles prayer and terror under a rain of jellied gasoline, "The Quaker Graveyard at Nantucket" takes off from the drowned body of a torpedoed sailor picked up off Mandaket, and "The Mills" is haunted by the memory of a husband invalided home with shellshock from Pearl Harbor. But this is all. Lowell's poetry is bookish in a sense; that is, it is saturated with Hawthorne and Melville, and other New England writers, especially Emerson, though the last is usually ironically paraphrased. And, as has been implied, it wears local history and tradition like a garment. Tremendously effective when he touches the ocean, Lowell is doubly so when he brings in, almost as a bass part to his melody, references to our reading of Ahab and the "Pequod." He all but brings the smell of salt air to one's nostrils. As religious verse, his compares with that of Hopkins; it is passionate as only that of a convert or mystic can be, yet it has a freedom as to topics and allusion ("St. Peter, the distorted key") that seems to the startled Protestant almost libertarian. At a hazard, the great poems are "The Quaker Graveyard," "In Memory of Arthur Winslow," "Salem," "Rebellion," "As a Plane Tree by the Water," "At the Indian Killer's Grave," and "Mother Marie Therese." But another time I might make another choice, I like so many.

Interviewed recently in London, Mr. T. S. Eliot lamented the fact that "there were so many American poets one had hopes of nine years ago, and nearly all of them seem to have spoilt their chances . . . by writing too much, exploiting themselves too recklessly, not stopping enough to think, not caring enough to prune." But he went on to say, "I must admit to a continuing respect for Robert Lowell and Richard Wilbur." And well he might, for each of these young men produced in his first volume more memorable poems than were found in the first volumes of Robinson, of Frost, and of—Eliot! And the case is not quite as bad elsewhere as Mr. Eliot indicates. The poets here glanced at provide the threshold for a new classicism.

AFTERWORD

This is what may be called a "stock-taking" essay—one in which either a scholar or critic forces himself to evaluate the better things which have been written in a given area in a specifically limited time. Fortunate is he who, through commission or in the regular course of his duties, has to do this kind of literary accounting once a year. The practice may be commended to the generality of writers, for it keeps one constantly on the alert for what is new and promising in literature, gives one an awareness without which the vision darkens and the veins thicken and close. Interest in youthful endeavor keeps one young, and surely it is better to be charged with adolescence than senility. In the "stock-taking" essay it is hardly ever a problem what to put in; it is what one has to leave out that causes anguish. I confess to liking this particular essay of ten years ago, because, given its space and time limitations, it was as good a summary as I have ever managed. It was not an easy essay to write, for we who had welcomed the great poetry renascence earlier in the century, who had danced delightedly in that deluge, have an inclination to believe that all American poetry was written then, which plainly just isn't so. Further, since my design was to interest new readers in current verse, I had to save space enough to advance the special talents of those whom I selected. The last thing a "stock-taking" essay should be is a mere enumeration—one is not dealing with the family budget. The strategy and pain impose themselves. Time and the votaries of poetry will do the auditing.

12 MASS MEDIA
AND LITERATURE

THE MASS MEDIA today appear to me either relatively apathetic or positively allergic to literature. Fifty years ago and within my memory, small city papers habitually printed fictional serials, and thus as a youth I became acquainted not only with *The Girl of the Limberlost, Alias Jimmy Valentine,* and "K" by Mary Roberts Rinehart, but also with *John Barleycorn* by Jack London and *Captains Courageous* by Kipling. This was not a high order of literature, I grant, but it was a demonstration of good will toward creative writing. Then came an era when, obese with advertising, these same papers went through the American fakery of reducing by eliminating excesses like fictional serials. The small suburban papers which keep them display a taste far beneath that of 1910 and cannot be said to be friendly to literature. The lordly *New York Times* still hospitably prints jingles which are submitted to it, but less than one per cent of these ever get into books of poetry, and even then, as contributions to literature, are on the dubious side.

Newspaper reviewing, a palpable witness to an interest in letters, is at an all-time low, with *The Times* deplorably setting the standard. Clifton Fadiman once defined book reviewing as merely a device for earning a living—"one of the many wierd results of Gutenberg's invention." He admitted that his definition was based on current practice, but that practice hasn't ostensibly changed in twenty years. Journalistic reviewers feel that they have adequately performed their function when they record the publication of a book as an event, without an indelicate inquiry into the volume's contents. If this is an adequate standard, none better achieves it than do Orville Prescott and Charles Poore in the daily *Times*. One admires Prescott's urbanity and Poore's unfailing wit (whatever the subject), but their reviews are transparently innocent of what most concerns creative writers at the moment. Disaffiliation, alienation, loneliness, traumas, crime, perversion occasionally shock them into writing sermons rather than reviews. Doubtless these are good for the very young who prefer *The Times* to any other reading. *The New York Times Book Review*, which most of us get on Sunday but which the advertisers get on Thursday, apparently measures the length of its reviews by the amount of space purchased by the respective publishers—at least there is a ratio between the two. Last month a congress of the editors of little magazines issued a manifesto attacking the choice of books reviewed and expressing doubt about the literary sensibility of its editor, Lewis Browne. But it may be said in defense of this periodical that rarely does an important book escape listing—it is the quality and relative weight of the reviews that are at fault. Anyone who reads the *London Times Literary Supplement* blushes for its American counterpart. To my knowledge there is no paper today with as consistently good reviews as were published in the *Boston Evening Transcript* or the *New York World* three decades ago. And where today in the newspapers are the likes of James Huneker, Heywood Broun, Floyd Dell, and Franklin P. Addams—men, who, if they liked a book or a play, would go all out for it and its author?

Those other news media, *Life*, *Time*, and their imitators, again treat the publication of a book or the opening of a play as a news event and occasionally do a feature article on a well-established author. None of them, so far as I know, has ever "discovered" a writer. *Time* chooses better the books and authors whom it notices than does *Newsweek* which must have established some sort of record for bad selection and dullness, but at least the reader is spared the notorious gavottes, prances, and *entrechats* of the regimented Luce style. Some of Dos Passos' and Hemingway's worst writing has appeared in *Life*, but magazines of this type, employing their large resources, occasionally bring together factual material which may be very useful if carefully checked. *Look*, for example, has published valuable materials on Faulkner's background, but no interview by any one of these periodicals has ever elicited the substance of those exemplary conversations which have appeared in the *Paris Review*. It ought to be within their powers, but isn't. Perhaps the interviewer, whatever his journalistic skill, should know something about the writer's work *and respect it*, before he begins. Perhaps it is the delicious sense of frustrated great power that makes the average reader rejoice at the failure of one of these magazines to succeed with J. D. Salinger, even though the rejoicing reader himself would like to know more about Salinger. Is it fair to say that, despite their endeavors, these particular media have done less for literature than *Esquire*, the *New Yorker*, and recently, *McCall's?*

One should not expect as much sympathy, quantitatively, for literature from the exploiters of film as from the exploiters of print, for the affinities exist mainly in the area of drama. Film has gone through such a tremendous evolution since *The Great Train Robbery* in 1905, the first connected dramatic narrative to be told on the screen, that it has never been a stable medium to which a true literary artist could commit himself wholeheartedly, though many have done so. The silent film, the interloping radio broadcast, the talkies, chromofilm, stereofilm, and television, overlapping each other within a generation, contain few names, besides those of actors, and few if any stars among the latter, who have survived all of these rapid transformations. The "classics" cited in the history of the silent film are chiefly creations for that film and not adaptations from literature; the Mack Sennett farces, the D. W. Griffith extravaganzas (with the exception of *The Birth of a Nation*, though its source was hardly literature), *The Cabinet of Dr. Caligari*, the work in Europe of such directors and producers as Lang, Murnau, Lubitsch, René

Clair, Kuleshov, Eisenstein, and Pudovkin is in the direction of creating a distinct medium with little reference to literature—as perhaps it should be. Indeed, the theoreticians of the thirties, like Arnheim and Spottiswood, cite the film performances, with the camera fixed at eye-level in the middle of the set and stationary, of *Queen Elizabeth* and *La Dame aux Camélias*, the only records we have of the immortal Sarah Bernhardt, as everything the cinema play should not be. But if literature had little effect upon the silent film, that film had definite effects upon literature. One need only mention how Charlie Chaplin became the idol of the Dadaists in Paris and how the expressionist film influenced the work of John Dos Passos and Clifford Odets, to make the point.

There was a time in the mid-thirties when it appeared that the poets might make a conquest of the radio drama. Going back to the twenties, I can remember when Carleton and Manley, members of the English department at New York University and graduates of the Harvard 47 Workshop, were pioneering on radio with the natural poetry of the Bible in half-hour dramas. Later, we had a department project to review books which became very burdensome (preparation for any of the mass media should not be a part-time enterprise). Then, after the failure of *Scribner's* magazine, Warren Bower began his weekly book reviews over WNYC, which are still on the air and have passed the 750 mark. Willis Wager and Henry Popkin, without his endurance, did similar reviewing in Boston.

But to return to the poetic drama. In the thirties, as I have said, there was an efflorescence of verse plays on radio. One recalls readily those of Alfred Kreymborg and Archibald MacLeish (the latter's *The Fall of the City*, based on F. D. R.'s Inaugural theme, "We have nothing to fear but fear itself," is both a radio and literary classic), such special things as Kimball Flaccus' *The Fulton Fish Market*, and poetry recitals by most of the leading poets of the day. The radio would seem ideally suited for poetic expression, but its ascendancy was too quickly interrupted by the rise of the talking film to allow for the development of radio literary artists, though the work of Norman Corwin in prose dramas survives to show us of what the medium is capable. The fact remains that literature had a warmer reception on radio than in the silent film. That it failed to perfect an art in that medium was due to no hostility, but to certain definite limitations of the writers themselves who could not subsist on what the medium paid and hopefully shifted with the public to other media.

The sound film, whether black and white, or chromatic, has been much more sympathetic to literature than was the silent film. Everyone can supplement from his own pleasurable experience my few citations of such sympathetic treatments of literary classics in the "talkies" as would have pleased the original authors. I think easily of Hugo's *The Hunchback of Notre Dame*, of Dostoevsky's *The Brothers Karamazov*, of Dickens' *David Copperfield* and *Bleak House*, of Henry James's *Washington Square*, of Stephen Crane's *The Bride Comes to Yellow Sky* and *The Red Badge of Courage*, of Lillian Hellman's *The Little Foxes*, of the Grimms' *Snow White and the Seven Dwarfs*, and of Jules Verne's *Around the World in Eighty Days*. The partial conversion of Hollywood to the faithful reproduction of literary classics was a slow and painful one—one recalls the lost suit of Theodore Dreiser over the butchery of *The American Tragedy*—but it was public opinion, the competition of British, French, and Italian films, and the success financially of the scripts that did not have to be altered, like *Quo Vadis* and *Ben Hur*, and *not* the protests of the authors and critics, which swayed Hollywood, still untrustworthy in its behavior. The filming of a book had an extraordinary effect on the sales of that book. There was an immediate and enormous demand after they were filmed for all the books I have cited. *King's Row* had sold only about 10,000 copies, according to Max Wylie, when it was filmed; thereupon it became one of the best sellers of the century. Unfortunately filming has also raised books that have the least perceptible merit, like *The Robe*, into enormous sellers.

The "talkies" have had less effect on the techniques of

poetry, drama, and fiction, than had the silent film, for fundamentally they have merely improved on devices, aside from sound, originated by the old movies. But Hollywood itself has become a literary subject for Bud Shulberg in *What Makes Sammy Run*, for Nathanael West in *The Day of the Locust* (with its interesting film technique), for F. Scott Fitzgerald in *The Last Tycoon*, and for Norman Mailer in *The Deer Park*. Hollywood has been receptive to not only the authors of these books, but writers like Odets, Herman Wouk, Tennessee Williams, and Irwin Shaw have written for it. I believe their employment there has been deleterious, but who can detect any influence, beneficial or otherwise, on the work of William Faulkner, who, I am told, is the author of seven scripts? So far as American literature is concerned, it seems as if about as many pluses as minuses could be scored for Hollywood. I am happy that today's program does not call upon me to estimate the effect of American movies abroad, for undeniably we have exported some of our worst films. I have never seen in a country village movie house in the U. S. in years such bad American films as I have seen in Paris and Mexico City.

Television, the inheritor of all that radio and film have learned or failed to learn, derived from radio a vice which the movies, in any form, never had to cope with—the commercial. Into the midst of any program may be intruded every ten minutes the most foreign matter imaginable, making a unity of impression impossible. I find even my interest in world news distracted in the Huntley-Brinkley report by my concern for the health of James Daly, the highest paid commercialist on TV, according to a Madison Avenue acquaintance. "Are you smoking more, but enjoying it less? . . . Have a real cigarette—have a Camel!" Big-hearted Ed Sullivan, who has given TV the equivalent of the B. F. Keith vaudeville show (which I used so much to enjoy), produced a special program for children this Christmas eve—and his sponsors were a cigaret and a lipstick. My parents would have found the conjunction immoral; I find it only incongruous. But even to me there is something odious in the quip, "Promise her anything but give her Arpege." To one viewer, at least, Arpege is forever Tabu.

Because of the commercials and because of TV's decision to emphasize half-hour (really twenty-minute) shows, the opportunity for good drama is at the minimum on television. Alfred Hitchcock seems to be about the only producer who can occasionally do well in that limited space, and I rejoice to learn that his time is to be extended to an hour next year. His production this week of Susan Glaspell's *A Jury of Her Peers* was not merely superb, but a miracle considering the time in which it was given. Back in 1953–54, when the magazines were still contesting for advertising, though *Collier's* was dying even then, as the *Post* appears to be today, and commercials were sparse, the playwright had the better part of an hour on the picture tube. The result was the appearance of a whole flock of promising young writers who fashioned their work, and some of it was excellent, solely for TV presentation: Robert Alan Aurthur, Paddy Chayefsky, Horton Foote, J. P. Miller, Tad Mosel, Reginald Rose, Rod Serling, and Gore Vidal. The last named expressed to me a considerable enthusiasm for television, with, however, this caveat: he said that he would much rather write for it than look at it. Even recently stations with limited commerical support have been able to present better drama programs than the big boys with the national hookups. Who of us, in the metropolitan area, was not grateful for "The Play of the Week" series on WNTA a year ago. Of course, there have been ambitious efforts to do justice to literature that have missed the mark, like the Esso-sponsored presentation of English history through Shakespeare, in which the clipped British speech and the effort to get in as much as possible defeated the endeavor. The tribute to Robert Frost, with a jigger of verse and a shaker of pictures, became laughable when a voice proclaimed "Whose woods these are . . ." and the camera man, unwilling to wade in deep snow, produced a picture of a broken-down apple orchard.

The general effect of a treatment of a work of literature

on TV is the same as the effect of a treatment by cinema—sales go up immediately. Right after World War II, Charles Laughton, who had been doing the same thing in army camps, brought about a revival of interest in Thomas Wolfe's prose by reading it on television. When Floyd Zulli lectured on Stendhal's *The Red and the Black* on Sunrise Semester, the demand was so great that not a copy of the novel remained unsold in the metropolitan area. Professor Baxter's lectures on Shakespeare had a similar result on the West Coast. Of course, there have been difficulties with censorship and senseless cutting and altering. The Ford Theatre decided that Donald Davidson's version of—of all things—of Henry James's *What Maisie Knew*—was "not in keeping with its obligation to the viewing public" and cancelled its agreement for the presentation of the show. Alfred Hitchcock has compiled a whole volume of excellent stories which he is not allowed to present. But this is a phase. The real villains are Madison Avenue and a weak-kneed Federal Communications Commission. Because commercials allow no time for character development and achievement of atmosphere, the producer is practically confined to crime films and Westerns because their action is so strongly melodramatic that it can be retained over the interruptions. The FCC seems unconcerned about the number of commercials that may be crowded into an hour's time; it has ignored the fraud of "station identification" notices which allow the station to crowd in as many as six commercials. We have just about concluded the worst year in TV history, yet I go along with Gore Vidal in trusting that television may yet be a benefaction to mankind and a medium for literature. It is the masters and not the medium's highly developed instruments and skills which frustrate it.

AFTERWORD

This is a talk I gave at the Hilton Hotel in New York on invitation by one of the speech associations in

December, 1961, and has not hitherto been published. I include it because it illustrates something in which I thoroughly believe: a critic or scholar should not limit his interests or activities wholly to a speciality but should range widely, even into areas unfamiliar to him, even into *terra incognita*. By no stretch of the imagination could I be called a specialist on the mass media. But who, save Gilbert Seldes, could be so designated? Newspapers and weeklies have specialists in the distinguishable media, but when do they ever get out of their columns or boxes? Whenever a writer spirals down in narrowing circles to a single subject, he narrows not only his vision but his very spirit. The greater moral health of the fiction writer is a consequence of the broad demands of his craft—the scholar or critic should imitate him and look about, even venture out. Instead of taking cold, he might get oxygen in his lungs, make the acquaintance of an idea or two. He will, of course, occasionally come a cropper, but he can get up and scramble on. A pluralistic critic should have pluralistic interests, and venturing is a way to get them.

Since I made these sincere but somewhat uncharitable observations, there have been some improvements in the mass media. *The New York Review*, for example, has been founded; in it, with Alfred Kazin establishing the tone and quality, reviews quite as thorough as those which the British enjoy in the *Times* and *Guardian* have appeared. *The New York Times Book Review* has improved its typography, perhaps an earnest of better things to come. There is much good music now over radio; the role of WQXR is no longer a nearly solitary one; opera is still broadcast every Saturday afternoon from the Metropolitan. *Tom Jones* was made into a superb film even if the end was tampered with. Such weekly television shows as *Mr. Novak* and *The Defenders* have an occasional offering that is challenging to the mind. And there has been a marked improvement in the filming of documentaries, as in Charles Boyer's narrative history of the Louvre. I should be sanguine.

INDEX

Abrams, M. H.: archetypes are not clarifying, 11

Adam Blair (J. G. Lockhart): contrasted with *The Scarlet Letter*, 77

Adams, C. F., Jr. (brother to H. Adams): war service, 38; conflicts with Henry, 41; interest in railroads, 41, 46; Harvard overseer, 46

Adams, Charles Francis: ambassador, 37–38; presidential aspirations, 40; embarrassed by Henry, 43; Harvard influence, 46

Adams, Henry: Norman delusion, 36–37; secretary to father, 37–40; diletantism, 37–44; ambitions as journalist, 41–42; equipment as historian, 44, 45–48; controversy with E. A. Freeman, 46–58; supporter of F. Palgrave, 46, 49–58; marriage, 49; as teacher, 55, 56–57, 59; in Washington, 59–62; novelist, 60–62; J.-K. Huysman's influence, 62–65, return to medievalism, 62–66; feminist, 66–67; racist, 68

Adams, Mrs. Henry (Marian Hooper): marriage, 49; discomforts E. A. Freeman, 57–58; relation to *Esther*, 60–62; suicide, 60–62; devotion to father, 61

Addams, F. P.: as reviewer, 172, 186

Afterword: to "Toward a Pluralistic Criticism," 15–16; to "Walt Whitman and *His Leaves of Grass*," 35; to "The Medievalism of Henry Adams," 67–68; to "William Dean Howells as Henry James's 'Moral Policeman,'" 94; to "*The Turn of the Screw* and Alice James," 116–17; to "A Robber Baron Revises *The Octopus*," 130; to "Mencken and the South," 140; to "Anatomist of Monsters," 152–53; to "Hart Crane in Limbo," 161–62; to "Mr. Eliot Regrets . . . ," 169; to "Poetry Since the Deluge," 183–84; to "Mass Media and Literature," 193

Aiken, Conrad: resemblance to R. P. Warren, 153

Alcoholism: H. Crane as a victim, 155

Alienation: characteristic of Southern writers, 153

Allen, Gay Wilson: on the mind of W. Whitman, 7

All the King's Men (R. P. Warren): parallels the story of Huey Long, 149–52; superiority to S. Lewis' *It Can't Happen Here* and